Cambridge Elements ≡

Elements in Public and Nonprofit Administration
edited by
Andrew Whitford
University of Georgia
Robert Christensen
Brigham Young University

GLOBAL CLIMATE GOVERNANCE

David Coen
University College London

Julia Kreienkamp
University College London

Tom Pegram
University College London

CAMBRIDGE
UNIVERSITY PRESS

University Printing House, Cambridge CB2 8BS, United Kingdom

One Liberty Plaza, 20th Floor, New York, NY 10006, USA

477 Williamstown Road, Port Melbourne, VIC 3207, Australia

314–321, 3rd Floor, Plot 3, Splendor Forum, Jasola District Centre,
New Delhi – 110025, India

79 Anson Road, #06–04/06, Singapore 079906

Cambridge University Press is part of the University of Cambridge.

It furthers the University's mission by disseminating knowledge in the pursuit of education, learning, and research at the highest international levels of excellence.

www.cambridge.org
Information on this title: www.cambridge.org/9781108972895
DOI: 10.1017/9781108973250

First published 2020

A catalogue record for this publication is available from the British Library.

ISBN 978-1-108-97289-5 Paperback
ISSN 2515-4303 (online)
ISSN 2515-429X (print)

Global Climate Governance

Elements in Public and Nonprofit Administration

DOI: 10.1017/9781108973250
First published online: November 2020

David Coen
University College London

Julia Kreienkamp
University College London

Tom Pegram
University College London

Author for correspondence: Tom Pegram, t.pegram@ucl.ac.uk

Abstract: Climate change is one of the most daunting global policy challenges facing the international community in the twenty-first century. This Element takes stock of the current state of the global climate change regime, illuminating scope for policymaking and mobilizing collective action through networked governance at all scales, from the subnational to the highest global level of political assembly. It provides an unusually comprehensive snapshot of policymaking within the regime created by the United Nations Framework Convention on Climate Change (UNFCCC), bolstered by the 2015 Paris Agreement, as well as novel insight into how other formal and informal intergovernmental organizations relate to this regime, including a sophisticated EU policymaking and delivery apparatus, already dedicated to tackling climate change at the regional level. It further locates a highly diverse and numerous non-state actor constituency, from market actors to NGOs to city governors, all of whom have a crucial role to play.

Keywords: global governance, climate change, global public policy, global public goods, multi-level governance, policy transfer, implementation, Paris Agreement

ISBNs: 9781108972895 (PB), 9781108973250 (OC)
ISSNs: 2515–4303 (online), 2515-429X (print)

Contents

1 Introduction

Climate change is one of the most daunting issues facing the international community in the twenty-first century. It is a global governance challenge par excellence, since the actions of all states, corporations and individuals in this domain often have transboundary consequences on all others regardless of territorial boundaries. The international community has made major strides towards tackling the issue since the early 1990s, including concerted efforts within the EU. However, multiple challenges continue to hinder the establishment of a comprehensive, integrated regime and institutional framework capable of effectively combating climate change. Despite ample scientific consensus that the effects of climate change are real and will have profoundly negative impacts on a range of global public goods, from security to trade, health and human rights, efforts to advance an ambitious policy response have fallen far short. The recent Paris Agreement has been hailed by some as 'a model for effective global governance in the twenty-first century' (Slaughter, 2015). However, for others, the voluntary nature of the agreement risks delivering 'appealing promises and renewed victory statements, only to prolong the waiting game' (Gollier and Tirole, 2015: 1). The stakes are as high as they get.

This Element maps the current state of the global climate change regime with a view to taking stock of recent rapid developments in scholarship and real-world events in a post-Paris Agreement era. It illuminates the scope for mobilizing collective action through political, institutional and social channels at all scales of governance, from the subnational to the highest global level of political assembly. It also provides a contemporary snapshot of the interstate regime created by the United Nations Framework Convention on Climate Change (UNFCCC), bolstered by the 2015 Paris Agreement, as well as summary insight into how other formal and informal intergovernmental organizations relate to this regime, including a sophisticated European Union (EU) apparatus already dedicated to tackling climate change at the regional level. It further locates a highly diverse and numerous non-state actor constituency, from market actors to non-governmental organizations (NGOs) to city governors, all of whom have a crucial role to play given the need for fundamental changes in how domestic societies are organized. We hope that this Element will provide the scholarly and general reader with a valuable entry point into key scholarship on global climate governance. It is also intended to serve as an exercise in clarifying complexity, providing the reader with a guide to what may, at first glance, be an almost overwhelmingly complex ecosystem of global climate political activity. As we embark on this crucial decade for averting catastrophic global warming, it is vital that policy-making on environmental protection is rooted in a deeper understanding of how international and transnational actors interact, not just at the interstate level, but in relationship to a much wider range of domestic actors who indelibly shape political, economic and social life.

At the global level, while the UNFCCC continues to serve as a coordinating focal point within UN structures, there remains no central core to the diverse public and private regulatory arrangements on climate change that have emerged over the past three decades. As Keohane and Victor (2011) observe, there is no single global regime for climate change but rather a regime complex, comprising an array of regulatory elements that are only very partially organized hierarchically. Nevertheless, key institutions operating across different sectors and levels of governance are loosely coupled under the UNFCCC. Indeed, as we document, the Paris Agreement has led to the formalization of non-state actor participation, including by showcasing the climate commitments of cities, regions, businesses and investors through the Non-state Actor Zone for Climate Action portal (NAZCA). It is vital in any mapping of the global climate change regime to give due attention to climate policy initiatives operating outside multilateral forums, with signs of growing coherence among sub- and non-state actors in the form of umbrella initiatives such as the Global Covenant of Mayors for Energy and Climate and the We Mean Business Coalition (Hale, 2016). As this Element documents, an operational turn towards implementation ensures that national policies are now a major focus of concern. The ambitious procedural obligations set by the Paris Agreement will demand rapid and coordinated (re)deployment of local institutional capacity, as well as the building of public support for policy change and mobilization of communities to take action themselves.

One of the most striking shifts has been the evolution of climate policy in China and the United States, prior to the election of Donald Trump. In November 2014, a US–China agreement to take joint action on climate change set the stage for the momentous 2015 Paris Agreement (The White House, 2014). In 2020, the global climate governance landscape looks quite different. While public opinion may give cause for optimism, the US government has served notice to quit the Agreement and is allied with other major fossil fuel producers – Russia and Saudi Arabia – in their efforts to water down effective climate change mitigation efforts. Five years is a long time in climate politics. The obstructive tactics of recalcitrant states were on display at COP-25 held in Madrid in December 2019, widely deemed a disappointment. And this was before the world was engulfed in a global pandemic. It is too early to tell what impact COVID-19 will have on the global climate change response. While UN Secretary-General António Guterres insists that the pandemic must usher in a 'new model of global governance ... to ensure that power, wealth, and opportunities are shared more broadly and fairly at the international level (UN Secretary General, 2020)', other observers are convinced that the pandemic will entrench 'the fundamental characteristics of geopolitics today', characterized by faltering global cooperation and increasingly antagonistic great-power rivalry (Haass, 2020). Nevertheless, Patricia Espinoza, the Executive Secretary of the UNFCCC insists that their work 'is not, in any form, on hold' (UNFCCC, 2020). Climate change governance is inevitably impacted by the power-political and organizational challenges posed by major member states which refuse to endorse the critical function of global governance structures in coordinating action on the climate emergency.

Ultimately, mobilizing cooperation on the myriad 'wicked problems' which comprise the climate challenge presents an unprecedented collective action problem, given that exacerbation of the risks arises directly out of both macro-environmental interdependence and countless micro-interactions, with virtually all individuals, often unaware, implicated in their intensification (Bernstein and Hoffman, 2019). In other words, not even the most powerful states (or international organizations) will be able to resolve this problem alone and could easily make the situation worse. Indeed, the COVID-19 pandemic has starkly demonstrated the fragility of global response structures and their limited effectiveness in managing such complex global catastrophic risks. It has also highlighted the dangers posed by the erosion of trust in scientific advice as well as national and international public authorities, exacerbated by exclusionary nationalist policies by some major powers and a cyber-enabled 'infodemic' of fake news (United Nations, 2020). In turn, as this Element highlights, agreeing upon the contours of 'the problem' posed by climate change is itself a challenging task. This matters. As policy scholars' flag, accurate problem identification is crucial to devising an appropriate governance response (Peters, 2005). We probe the problem identification challenge through a novel examination of the global public goods dimensions of climate change governance. General agreement that a safe and relatively stable climate is a vital global public good belies the relative lack of consensus over how the problem of climate change should be understood, what must be done, and by whom – with important consequences for which kind of actors get to participate in climate governance processes.

Our mapping of the global climate change regime complex provides an unusually comprehensive insight into how a multilateral architecture of systems-wide principles, rules and procedures is being reshaped to serve as a stable evolving framework capable of accommodating the dynamism of global public policymaking and delivery in the new century (Coen and Pegram, 2018). Designing and enabling responses to climate change will require broad goal-setting, supplemented by rapid and strategic experimentation by many decentralized actors cognizant of the opportunities and challenges posed by their own operational contexts. This experimental approach is well captured by Hale's (2017) framing of the Paris Agreement as embracing a 'catalytic' model of cooperation, breaking with the legacy 'regulatory' approach. In turn, we complement this notion of a 'catalytic' UNFCCC regime with Keohane and Victor's (2011) framing of a global regime complex. Importantly, we also explore a novel extension of global governance through the creation of independent national climate advisory bodies as a viable pathway to global-to-local climate policy implementation. Given the vast scale of the global climate change regime complex, combined with the absence of any central data repository to account for all regime participants, data collection relies largely on desk research surveying academic literature and policy reports, relevant websites, as well as online data collections, including the International Environmental Agreements (IEA) Database Project.

This Element begins by defining global climate change governance before turning to an analysis of its global public goods dimensions. It then provides an overview of the historical development of the global climate change regime which has resulted in the Paris Agreement. This is followed by a summary mapping of actors involved in global climate change governance. Finally, the analysis locates these diverse actors within the context of an increasingly integrated global regime complex, spotlighting emergent coordinated efforts to accelerate implementation of global climate policy within domestic political jurisdictions. This sets the scene for future work on independent climate advisory bodies, as well as the role of the private sector in limiting warming to a 1.5 °C limit.

2 What Is Global Climate Change Governance?

Before embarking on a domain-mapping exercise, it is important to be explicit on the definitional boundaries of that domain. Climate change has emerged as a priority issue within the broader framework of global environmental governance over the past four decades. Pluralization of authority beyond the nation state is a key feature of this domain, where 'reconfiguration of authority across various actors and multiple levels of decision-making' is a longstanding feature (Hickmann, 2017). More broadly, scholarly efforts to grapple with a globalizing climate governance arena exemplify a rapidly developing cross-disciplinary convergence across a highly diverse body of social, technical and geophysical scholarship (Coen and Pegram, 2018). However, as a useful point of departure, global climate change governance can be defined generally as, 'all purposeful mechanisms and measures aimed at steering social systems towards preventing, mitigating, or adapting to the risks posed by climate change, established and implemented by states or other authorities' (Jagers and Stripple, 2003: 385).

A focus on 'all purposeful mechanisms and measures', as well as the implementation prerogatives of 'states or other authorities' provides the coordinates for this Element's mapping exercise. We build upon this definition by differentiating among key definitional elements along the dimensions of types of actors (state and non-state), scales of governance (global-to-local), as well as functional domains (regime complexes). The concept of regime complex has become a prominent lens through which to examine increasingly dense clusters of 'partially overlapping and non-hierarchical institutions governing a particular issue-area' (Raustiala and Victor, 2004: 279). Climate change is no exception. The UNFCCC-centred multilateral system constitutes an international regime in and of itself, understood as 'principles, norms, rules and decision-making procedures around which actors' expectations converge in a given area of international relations' (Krasner, 1982: 186). However, it also forms part of a larger *regime complex for climate change* spanning diverse formal and informal arrangements (e.g. private regulations, clubs, transnational initiatives) operating within this issue-area which together constitute a system of loosely coupled regulatory elements that are only partially organized hierarchically (Keohane and Victor, 2011: 12). Crucially, understanding climate change as a regime complex acknowledges that international institutions are themselves embedded within broader institutional frameworks. Opening up inquiry into the causes and consequences of overlaps and intersections among different regimes with an authority claim for a particular issue area (or territory) presents a significant departure from earlier work which tended to focus on discrete regimes ostensibly designed to govern discrete problems (Alter and Raustiala, 2018: 330).

As the concept of regime complex makes clear (see later discussion in Section 6.1), the problems posed by climate change go far beyond environmental governance which can be understood more narrowly as 'directed towards a range of causes – including conservation and environmental protection, spatial and land use planning, (sustainable) management of natural resources, and the protection of human health' (Challies and Newig, 2019). As van Asselt (2011: 59) observes, '[b]ecause of the intricate connections between climate change and other issue areas, there are interrelationships between the global climate regime and other areas of international law.' If we look at climate change regulation, as Wirth (2015) has suggested, important advances could be made quickly if the World Trade Organization (WTO) moved decisively to ensure that custom duties at the border accurately reflected the true environmental costs of goods. However, these interrelationships have only recently begun to receive academic attention, let alone been subject to effective supranational coordination (Gehring and Faude, 2013).

Finally, fragmentation has been identified as 'one of the fundamental problems of our current regime of global environmental governance' and is a recurring feature of this analysis (Esty, 2009: 427). The possible outcomes of fragmentation (as opposed to integration) of the global climate governance architecture has become a key focus of debate for both scholars and practitioners (Biermann et al., 2009; Isailovic et al., 2013). One frequently highlighted consequence of fragmentation is that responsibility for environmental issues is widely dispersed among different authority structures resulting in suboptimal policy coordination (Esty, 2009). For example, despite some obvious links and issue crossovers, 'the evolving regimes for climate change and biological diversity have little in common' (Young, 2008: 18). 'There are too many organizations engaged in environmental governance in too many different places, often with duplicative mandates' (Najam, Papa and Taiyab, 2006: 14). Beyond definitional boundaries or the functional challenge of effectively coordinating within such a dense actor ecosystem, as the next section makes clear, climate governance also confronts different views regarding its global public goods dimensions, with important distributive and normative consequences.

3 The Global Public Goods Dimensions of Climate Change Governance

A safe and relatively stable climate is now widely considered a vital global public good that requires global collective action. Global public goods (GPGs) are goods whose benefits or costs are of nearly universal reach or potentially affecting anyone anywhere. Arguably, most 'contemporary global challenges tend to possess the properties of a [GPG], or at least include components of a GPG nature' (Kaul and Blondin, 2016: 32). Although there are some GPGs that are naturally available (e.g. the oceans), many are human-made (e.g. the rules governing global trade or the international communication infrastructure). The latter include not just tangible goods or resources but also governance frameworks – including rules, norms and policies – that aim to address common global challenges. Just as 'publicness' is not a static category, 'globalness' is not always a 'natural, persistent property' (Kaul et al., 2003: 10). In other words, states often make political decisions about how 'public' or 'global' a particular good is. To explore the contested boundaries of GPGs in climate change governance, we interrogate three of the core objectives which inform the UNFCCC regime (for a summary, see Table 1 at the end of this section):

Table 1 Global public goods (GPG) dimension of climate change governance.

	Mitigation	Adaptation	Loss and damage (L&D)
GPG dimension widely acknowledged?	Yes, explicit in Convention	No: both the 'public' and the 'global' nature of adaptation remain contested	No: fundamental lack of agreement on what kind of 'good' L&D responses should produce
Main GPG provided?	Climate stability	Global climate resilience	Depending on frame: Global climate risk resilience *or* global justice
GPG clearly defined?	Yes: Paris Agreement sets goal of limiting global warming to well below 2 °C and ideally 1.5 °C	No: Paris Agreement sets goal of 'enhancing adaptive capacity, strengthening resilience and reducing vulnerability to climate change' but unclear what exactly that means and how progress can be measured (UNFCCC, 2015)	No: Paris Agreement recognizes 'importance of averting, minimizing and addressing loss and damage', however, states have very different interpretations of what that means in practice (UNFCCC, 2015)
Other GPG relevant policy objectives (or co-benefits)?	Mitigation has a range of GPG co-benefits, such as reduced dependence on fossil fuels, reduction of pollution, health benefits, etc.	Adaptation is also addressed in the context of sustainable development as well as disaster risk management	Discussions on L&D frequently spill over into adaptation, sustainable development and disaster risk management

Table 1 (cont.)

	Mitigation	Adaptation	Loss and damage (L&D)
	Across all three domains, data and knowledge production/sharing on climate change and appropriate responses also constitutes co-benefits with GPG character		
Historical importance?	Recognized as main objective from the beginning. As mitigation goals become less realistic, more emphasis being placed on adaptation and, more recently, L&D	Recognized from the beginning but largely sidelined for the first decade of the UNFCCC process. Adaptation and mitigation now formally enjoy equal importance; however, policy practice remains biased towards mitigation	Only very recently implicitly recognized as a 'third pillar' of the global climate regime; still not a priority issue during international climate negotiations
Source of contestation?	Equity and differentiation (fair burden-sharing); emissions accounting	Disproportionate focus on mitigation over adaptation; lack of sufficient funding for adaptation	Problem framing (recognition of L&D as completely distinct from adaptation; risk management and insurance vs liability and compensation); complete lack of funding for L&D
	Strong North-South division runs through all three domains but is probably most pronounced in the case of L&D		

- Climate change mitigation (stabilization of greenhouse gas concentration in the atmosphere)
- Climate change adaptation (enhancing adaptive capacity, strengthening resilience and reducing vulnerability to climate change)
- Climate change loss and damage (distributive or corrective justice through liability and compensation for climate change impacts)

It is important to note that there is no consensus on the boundaries, substance, distinctiveness or relative importance of these three domains. The international climate change regime remains primarily focused on mitigation, corresponding to an increasingly sophisticated institutional apparatus under the UNFCCC. Although the need for adaptation has informed international climate negotiations from the very beginning, it was only in the early 2000s that it emerged as a widely accepted policy objective (Schipper, 2006). Indeed, many initially considered adaptation a 'taboo', arguing that a focus on coping with climate change would distract from and weaken mitigation efforts (Pielke et al., 2007). Today, mitigation and adaptation are widely recognized as complimentary rather than dichotomous. Yet, as explored in the following, the GPG dimensions of adaptation remain contested and discussions under the UNFCCC continue to frame it 'as an exclusively local-to-national issue' (Benzie et al., 2018: 7). The limited success of both mitigation and adaptation efforts under the UNFCCC has led climate vulnerable countries to increasingly emphasize loss and damage (L&D) – the need to address unavoidable and unmanageable climate change impacts – as a separate policy objective. With the adoption of the Paris Agreement, L&D has been elevated, at least on paper, to 'a third pillar of international climate change law' (Broberg, 2020: 528). However, it continues to provoke controversy among negotiating parties due to its ambiguous definition and its emphasis on distributive and corrective justice.

A discussion of mitigation, adaptation and L&D as separate policy objectives allows us to place a spotlight on different conceptualizations of GPGs: What 'goods' should be provided? By whom? How 'global' or 'public' are these goods? What role does justice play? This provides vital context to the mapping of actors, mechanisms and processes of climate governance found in this Element. While analytic description of form, function, mechanisms and procedures provides valuable empirical insight into the workings of global governance, it is also important that global policy scholars do not lose sight of the deeper governance challenges posed by underlying distributive and normative implications of internationally agreed standards. Importantly, the different GPG implications of mitigation, adaptation and L&D do not justify siloed policy approaches. As explored in Sections 3.1–3.3, the three domains are closely linked and often hard to delineate, also spill over into issue areas such as sustainable development or disaster risk reduction. They present both synergies and potential trade-offs, calling for integrated perspectives and policy approaches that are sensitive to the multidimensional, multi-scalar nature of climate change (Thornton and Comberti, 2017).

3.1 GPG Domain #1: Climate Change Mitigation

Climate change mitigation is the original key objective of the UNFCCC regime. Global mitigation efforts can either be framed as preventing a global public 'bad' – climate change – or providing a global public 'good' – climate stability. Importantly, what constitutes 'dangerous climate change' or a 'stable climate' is ultimately a political decision. Under the 2015 Paris Agreement, governments have set the goal of limiting global warming to well below 2 °C above pre-industrial levels and pursue efforts towards a 1.5 °C limit, but experts warn that even global warming of 1.5 °C would pose serious risks for natural and human systems (IPCC, 2018a).

Human-induced climate change is widely recognized as a GPG problem par excellence. Climate change stability is not a GPG that is 'nice to have'; it is essential for human survival and it provides the basis for the provision of other GPGs such as biodiversity preservation or the containment of infectious dis-eases. Global warming also poses significant second-order threats to the legit-imacy and stability of governance systems more generally. Conversely, climate change mitigation can generate economic, environmental, social and political/ institutional innovations and secondary benefits which might constitute (global) public goods in themselves. Such 'co-benefits' of mitigation policies, implying 'a "win-win" strategy to address two or more goals with a single policy measure', have now become a central concept in academia and policy (Mayrhofer and Gupta, 2016: 22). They include, for example, the reduction of pollution and improvements of local air quality through decarbonization, which in turn provide huge health co-benefits. Mitigation measures are increasingly pitched to developing countries as win-win opportunities; reducing their dependence on imported fossil fuels, enhancing fiscal stability, providing green jobs and promoting technology transfer and investment (Mayrhofer and Gupta, 2016).

A stable climate is sometimes considered a pure GPG with non-excludable and non-rival properties: nobody can be excluded from enjoying its benefits and one person's consumption does not diminish the amount available to others. However, as the climate system is reaching key tipping points, it is more appropriate to conceptualize the climate, or, more precisely, the global sinks for greenhouse gases (GHGs), as a global common-pool resource rather than a pure public good (Ostrom et al., 1999; Cole, 2015; Paavola, 2019). Strong incentives to free-ride exist because the global carbon budget is finite but non-excludable and the costs and benefits of reducing GHG emissions are not directly linked. For this reason, climate change mitigation has been called 'the largest collective action problem that humanity has ever faced' (Jamieson, 2014: 104), a 'market failure on the greatest scale the world has seen' (Stern, 2007: 27) and the 'ultimate tragedy of the commons' (Paavola, 2012: 417). However, Brown, Adger and Cinner (2019) have warned that there might be dangers in overemphasizing the framing of climate change as a 'tragedy' as this may limit possibilities to change governance systems and mobilize moral values to achieve effective collective action on climate change. Aklin and Mildenberger (2018) argue that distributional conflicts on the national level pose a more significant governance dilemma than the danger of states free-riding on the efforts of others. Others question the dominant state-centrism of collective action problem frames, given that a handful of private 'carbon majors' are directly responsible for the majority of global industrial GHG emissions over the past three decades (Grasso and Vladimirova, 2020).

Climate change is a 'super-wicked' GPG problem (Levin et al., 2012), not just because of its planetary scale and potentially catastrophic impact but also because climate change displays some dynamics that make it especially difficult to address. Climate change is a highly complex problem that includes consider-able uncertainties, emergent properties and 'wild card' risks that could trigger sudden and non-linear changes and make mitigation exponentially more diffi-cult over time (Harrison and Geyer, 2019). In addition, it demands sacrifices from the current generation to safeguard GPG provision for future generations (Johnson and Levin, 2009) and there is only a very limited time frame left for this to happen (IPCC, 2018a). Indeed, some scholars argue that the super-wicked nature of the problem demands that analysts rethink framing it as a collective action problem (emissions reductions) or the preservation of a global commons (a stable biosphere) and instead understand it as a fractal phenomenon requiring attention at multiple scales to enable transformative pathways towards decarbonization (Bernstein and Hoffman, 2019). Such a profound conceptual shift is necessary, they argue, to accommodate an emerging 'politics of decarbonization' which inevitably has far-reaching and radical implications for 'changes in social, technical, economic, and political systems that underpin modern societies' (Bernstein and Hoffman, 2018: 191).

Although climate stability is a non-excludable GPG, the effects of under-provision are unevenly distributed geographically and demographically. Not only are most developing countries already at a geographic disadvantage, their economies and public infrastructures are especially vulnerable to the effects of climate change and they lack resources for adaptation, as will be discussed. Thus, 'the poorest countries and people will suffer earliest and most' (Stern, 2007: vii). This raises important problems of interstate justice as well as further problems for GPG provision as many of the biggest emitters will be least or last affected by the consequences of their action. Conversely, the 'contributions' to climate change are also uneven, with the major emitters comprising a fairly small group of countries and large corporations (Taylor and Watts, 2019). This poses an opportunity to the extent that GPG delivery can be facilitated through collective action among this core group of polluters (Grasso and Roberts, 2014). However, such optimism must confront a hard reality: that the costs of action are concentrated on a few powerful actors who are unwilling to shoulder them despite compelling evidence that the cost of inaction poses a catastrophic systemic risk, including for the asset management industry (The Economist, 2015).

Ultimately, climate change mitigation is an aggregate effort GPG that requires a broad cooperative effort for effective provision (Barrett, 2007). However, GPG provision is exceptionally costly and clashes with the preferences of entrenched public and private sector interest groups. This is exemplified by the political lock on the 'rapid and far-reaching transitions in energy, land, urban infrastructure (including transport and building) and industrial systems' which the Intergovernmental Panel on Climate Change (IPCC) has concluded are urgently required if global warming is to be limited to the 'safe' threshold of 1.5 °C (IPCC, 2018a: 17). As the Co-Chair of IPCC Working Group III acknowledges, 'limiting warming to 1.5 °C is possible within the laws of chemistry and physics but doing so would require unprecedented changes' (IPCC, 2018b). In the face of insufficient government commitment, private sector action may provide one of the most promising opportunities to drive forward effective climate change mitigation (Vandenbergh and Gilligan, 2017).

Other non-state actors from civil society organizations to cities also play an increasingly important role, by taking mitigation action themselves or by pushing for more ambitious pledges from governments and business leaders. Thus, provision of GPGs in this domain is not exclusively 'public.' Mitigation action by decentralized non-state actors poses its own collective problems, as well as risks. This is exemplified by the growing research and policy interest in geoengineering as a deliberate and potentially cost-effective way of stabilizing the Earth's climate (Dunne, 2018). While some scientists argue for 'properly designed field-experiments of limited duration and scale' (Blackstock et al., 2009: 38), others caution 'that real-world experimentation actually becomes deployment' with unpredictable consequences (ETC Group, 2009). Notwithstanding, the United States and Saudi Arabia are reportedly blocking global regulation of geoengineering (Watts, 2019). As global emissions continue to rise, large-scale decentralized deployment of geoengineering technology could become inevitable despite the risks posed, posing novel challenges for state authority and GPG delivery (Reynolds and Wagner, 2018).

3.2 GPG Domain #2: Climate Change Adaptation

The 2015 Paris Agreement sets an explicit long-term goal 'of enhancing adaptive capacity, strengthening resilience and reducing vulnerability to climate change, with a view to contributing to sustainable development and ensuring an adequate adaptation response' in the context of the Agreement's mitigation goal (UNFCCC, 2015). It also introduces regular adaptation communications and stronger procedural commitments on adaptation under the transparency framework and the global stocktake (a five-yearly review of collective progress towards the goals of the Agreement). However, the African Group failed to insert a new agenda item at COP-25 in Madrid to further define the global goal on adaptation. Both the academic literature and global policy discussion remain strongly biased towards mitigation and only a tiny fraction of global climate finance is currently spent on adaptation (Antonich, 2019). There are few legally binding provisions on adaptation, and they display a low degree of precision and obligation (Bodansky, 2016; Hall and Persson, 2018). With regard to actual implementation of adaptation action, the Agreement provides little substance and support, the focus being 'once again on planning, assessing, sharing information and reporting' (Sharma, 2017: 38). In sum, climate change adaptation still appears to be 'the overlooked cousin of greenhouse gas mitigation' (Schipper, 2006: 82).

An important reason for the under-provision of adaptation governance on the global level is that the GPG dimensions of adaptation are contested (Hall and Persson, 2018; Persson, 2019). As Ayers (2011: 62) notes, a key paradox of global adaptation governance is that 'climate change is a global risk, yet vulnerability is locally experienced.' Thus, the immediate benefits of adaptation measures are local rather than global. Flood defences, for example, clearly are public (non-rival and non-excludable) goods, yet their scope is limited: improving dams in the Netherlands will do nothing to enhance the resilience of coastal communities in India. In addition, the benefits of adaptation measures are not always purely public. For example, private individuals may choose to take measures to protect their houses from extreme weather events and farmers may switch to better irrigation systems in order to maximize private profit. For these reasons, climate change adaptation has traditionally not been considered to provide any GPGs and the need for global action has consequently been de-emphasized (Pickering and Rübbelke, 2014; Hall and Persson, 2018).

However, as mitigation strategies are falling dramatically short and adaptation to climate change impacts is becoming increasingly urgent, this view is now slowly shifting. The Paris Agreement defines adaptation as 'a global challenge faced by all with local, sub-national, national, regional and international dimensions' (UNFCCC, 2015). Global adaptation governance can help produce a range of GPGs that can be collectively framed as 'global climate resilience'. First, enhanced international cooperation and better funding for adaptation *directly* provides public goods that can be enjoyed globally, including improved climate models, knowledge sharing platforms and research on new emergent technologies such as drought-resistant crops.[1] Second, local adaptation measures have *indirect* effects that can be framed as GPGs, including the prevention of climate change-related displacement, the containment of infectious diseases or the enhancement of food security (Biermann and Boas, 2010). Third, adaptation measures can have important co-benefits for mitigation.[2] For example, mangrove restoration for flood protection also helps rebuilding crucial carbon sinks as mangroves are particularly effective at carbon sequestration.

Even where benefits are largely local and/or largely private, adaptation is likely to be underprovided without effective international cooperation (Magnan and Ribera, 2016). At present, the UNFCCC regime is channelling some resources towards adaptation through the Green Climate Fund (GCF), the Adaptation Fund, the Special Climate Change Fund (SCCF) and the Least Developed Countries Fund (LDCF). However, the bulk of climate finance provided by developed countries still aims at mitigation. Why is this? Unlike mitigation, adaptation is still not widely considered a GPG and adaptation finance is seen to provide an exclusive benefit for recipient countries (Odionu, 2019). Another reason is that 'adaptation finance raises some entirely new justice issues' (Ciplet, Roberts and Khan, 2013: 53), including discussions on historical responsibilities that developed countries would rather avoid.

Building on Kaul (2008), climate change adaptation can be conceptualized as a contested GPG that is marked by low 'publicness' – that is, 'globalness' – in utility but high publicness in provision. Global governance is crucial to make sure adaptation is adequately supplied; however, the immediate net-benefits are not distributed evenly around the globe. A stronger framing of adaptation as a GPG with long-term benefits for all could help channel more resources towards this domain. However, there is a danger that functional arguments which stress the indirect mutual benefits of adaptation crowd out arguments that build on notions of justice, equity and fairness. Such arguments emphasize that countries and communities which have contributed least to climate change will suffer most and bear the highest costs for adaptation. For them,

---

[1] It should, however, be noted that ostensibly 'global' knowledge does not automatically provide equal benefits for everyone (Johnson and Rampini, 2017).

[2] Conversely, adaptation activities may also negatively affect mitigation and vice versa.

international adaptation support does not so much provide 'net-benefits' but rather a limited form of compensation for the costs they have to incur as a result of climate change.

3.3 GPG Domain #3: Climate Change Loss and Damage

There is now overwhelming evidence that human-induced climate change is already happening and that current adaptation efforts are insufficient to prevent or alleviate all adverse impacts (IPCC, 2018a). The term loss and damage (L&D) usually refers to these 'residual' impacts. A major problem for any discussion in this domain is that there are competing views on what L&D actually is and how it should best be addressed. Broadly speaking, there are two distinct frames (Vanhala and Hestbaek, 2016; Schinko, Mechler and Hochrainer-Stigler, 2019). The first emphasizes that L&D is beyond adaptation and calls for liability and compensation. This frame has been advanced by developing countries, in particular Small Island Developing States, since the early days of the UNFCCC regime. Industrialized countries have strongly rejected this frame which highlights their historic responsibilities and the need for distributive and corrective justice. In response, they have sought to frame L&D as essentially equivalent to adaptation or as a case for comprehensive risk management and insurance-based solutions.

This fundamental tension has never been resolved even as L&D became more institutionalized within the UNFCCC. It first entered the official UNFCCC agenda in 2007, with the Bali Action Plan calling for action on '[d]isaster reduction strategies and means to address loss and damage associated with climate change impacts in developing countries that are particularly vulnerable to the adverse effects of climate change' (UNFCCC, 2008). But it was not until 2013 that a dedicated institutional arrangement on L&D was established: the Warsaw Mechanism on Loss and Damage (WIM). The WIM has three main functions, namely: (1) enhancing knowledge and understanding on L&D, (2) strengthening dialogue, and (3) enhancing action and support, including with regard to finance, technology and capacity-building. By devoting an entire article to L&D, the 2015 Paris Agreement firmly anchors this issue as a permanent item on the agenda of international negotiations, implicitly recognizing it as a 'third pillar' of international climate policy distinct from adaptation. However, the accompanying Paris Decision explicitly states that this does not provide any basis for liability and compensation (UNFCCC, 2016).

Despite this milestone achievement, the debate on L&D remains 'broad, diffuse and somewhat confusing' (Mechler et al., 2019: 4). The ambiguity of L&D as a concept complicates the discussion of its GPG dimensions. There is fundamental disagreement about what kind of 'good' a global governance framework for L&D should ideally provide. Therefore, L&D is not usually viewed through a GPG lens. Nevertheless, L&D provides a challenging case study of a governance problem which displays two competing GPG frames: 'global climate risk resilience' vs. 'global justice'.

Global climate risk resilience. While the immediate benefits of L&D responses are primarily local and not purely public, aggregate and indirect effects constitute GPGs that provide mutual, if uneven, gains such as 'more resilient global supply chains, reduction of climate refugees and enhanced security' (Calliari, Surminski and Mysiak, 2019: 174). Locally implemented comprehensive climate risk management strategies will ultimately make the whole world more resilient. In addition, international cooperation on L&D can create institutional arrangements and knowledge-sharing platforms with GPG character, such as the UNFCCC clearinghouse for risk transfer (UNFCCC Clearinghouse, n.d.). Insurance and other risk pooling initiatives may also constitute public goods, although such mechanisms do not currently exist on the global level.

Global climate justice. In contrast, as approached by vulnerable developing countries and a growing number of civil society organizations, L&D focuses primarily on distributive and corrective justice. Both can be conceptualized as a GPG. As Kapstein (1999) argues, distributive justice (i.e. efforts to reconcile efficiency and fairness in the global economy) has long been recognized as a GPG, central to enhancing global economic and political stability. Indeed, distributive justice principles are already established under the UNFCCC regime, including the need for developed countries to provide financial and technical support for mitigation and adaptation action in developing countries. Yet, corrective justice mechanisms such as financial 'compensations' for L&D are currently not a politically viable solution. Financial compensation is also unlikely to adequately address the devastating implications of irreversible L&D for 'more intangible losses, such as loss of community, sovereignty, and mental health' (James, Jones and Boyd, 2017).

As Johnson and Rampini (2017: 271) note, GPG concepts do not usually 'distinguish *between* the various publics that may benefit under different conditions, nor [do they] suggest how we might evaluate which publics should be prioritized.' An excessive focus on risk reduction and risk transfer is not only inappropriate when it comes to addressing slow-onset impacts, it also obscures questions of justice and responsibility. On the other hand, 'framing L&D exclusively in terms of justice might have turned the issue into a win-lose negotiation game' (Calliari, Surminski and Mysiak, 2019: 174). Although these two frames need not be mutually exclusive, a reconciliation appears unlikely. Innovative finance mechanisms (such as a global fossil fuel extraction levy, a global carbon tax, etc.) could provide an alternative way to gather funds for loss and damage; however, they encounter significant political resistance (Roberts et al., 2017).

Although its inclusion in the Paris Agreement is of major symbolic importance, L&D is still not a priority issue during international climate negotiations. In the absence of any concrete funding commitments, hardly any progress has been made on the third function of the WIM – enhancing action and support for L&D. The most recent review of the WIM at COP-25 failed to encourage new streams of finance, making the mechanism 'a car without fuel' in the eyes of vulnerable countries (Basu, 2019). As the next section documents, the historical development of the climate change regime has been marked by sharp disagreements, as ill-equipped multilateral venues wrestle with the 'four-dimensional spaghetti' of competing demands provoked by climate negotiations (Carbon Brief, 2018). As L&D demonstrates, those on the frontline of climate impacts, such as local and indigenous communities, as well as small-island nations, have struggled to galvanize meaningful action through the UNFCCC process.

4 Overview: Historical Development of the Climate Change Regime

Despite its obvious GPG dimensions, the climate is a relatively new concern for global governance. The results of three decades of interstate discussion, negotiation and ratification on effective climate change policy implementation are underwhelming. Nevertheless, the 2015 Paris Agreement has injected new vigour into the imperative of tackling the climate emergency. In the words of one observer, 'while it [the Paris Agreement] didn't save the planet, it may have saved the chance to save it – that is, it didn't foreclose the possibility' (Bill McKibben qtd in E360, 2015).

4.1 The Evolution of the UNFCCC Regime

In the second half of the twentieth century, climate change – initially a purely scientific concern – gradually entered the wider international public and political debate. The first global conference on the environment was held in Stockholm in 1972. However, it took until 1988 before the first intergovernmental organization explicitly devoted to assessing the dangers posed by climate change was established: the Intergovernmental Panel on Climate Change (IPCC). The IPCC's First Assessment Report, released in 1990, confirmed that the world is warming and that 'emissions resulting from human activities are substantially increasing the atmospheric concentrations of the greenhouse gases', leading to further warming of the Earth's surface (IPCC, 1990: 63). The work of the IPCC helped convince UN member states to launch negotiations on an international treaty to address climate change (Weart, 2008). After two years of negotiations, the United Nations Framework Convention on Climate Change (UNFCCC) was adopted at the 1992 Earth Summit in Rio de Janeiro, along with its sister conventions on biological diversity and desertification.

Like many other international environmental agreements, the UNFCCC design follows a 'framework convention plus' model (Bodansky, Brunnée and Rajamani, 2017: 104). Thus, the Convention itself was kept largely procedural in nature and its substantial provisions were formulated in rather vague language. Article 2 of the Convention defined the ultimate objective of the global climate change regime, namely the 'stabilization of greenhouse gas concentrations in the atmosphere at a level that would prevent dangerous anthropogenic interference with the climate system' (United Nations, 1992). Beyond this, the Convention left specific targets and timetables to be set in subsequent treaties. However, Article 3 laid out a number of principles that should guide its implementation, including the consequential obligation of parties to take action 'on the basis of equity and in accordance with their common but differentiated responsibilities and respective capabilities' (United Nations, 1992). Reflecting this principle – often abbreviated as CBDR-RC – the Convention divided parties into 'Annex I' (developed) and 'non-Annex I' (developing) countries, with the former expected to 'take the lead in combating climate change and the adverse effects thereof' (United Nations, 1992).

The CBDR-RC principle was strongly reflected in the Kyoto Protocol, adopted at the third meeting of the Conference of the Parties (COP-3) in 1997. Modelled on the uniquely successful 1987 Montreal Protocol on Substances that Deplete the Ozone Layer, the Kyoto Protocol embodied a prescriptive top-down approach (Held and Roger, 2018). It was the first international treaty to establish binding GHG emissions reduction targets, with Annex-I countries accepting differentiated targets to reduce their overall emissions by 'at least 5 per cent below 1990 levels in the commitment period 2008 to 2012' (UNFCCC, 1998). However, it excluded non-Annex I countries from any mitigation commitments, even voluntary ones (Held and Roger, 2018). After the adoption of the Kyoto Protocol, many of its operational details still needed to be finalized. However, developing the Kyoto 'rulebook' proved contentious, especially after the United States, under the newly elected George W. Bush, announced its intention not to ratify (Bäckstrand and Elgström, 2013). Nevertheless, under leadership of the EU, the remaining parties managed to reach a compromise on the rulebook at COP-7 in Marrakech in 2001. Four years later, ratification by Russia finally set the Kyoto Protocol into effect (Oberthür, 2011).

Once the Kyoto Protocol had entered into force, a key question was what the post-2012 international climate regime would look like. At COP-11 in Montreal, parties launched a dual-track negotiation process. One track (the 'Kyoto track') focused on reaching agreement on a second commitment period for Annex I parties under the Kyoto Protocol; the other (the 'UNFCCC track') was initially an informal process to discuss wider options for future climate action by all parties. At COP-13 in Bali, parties adopted the Bali Action Plan, thus formalizing UNFCCC track negotiations for a more inclusive post-Kyoto treaty, with many expecting that the two negotiation tracks would be unified in 2009, at COP-15 in Copenhagen, leading to a new, legally binding agreement (von Bassewitz, 2013). COP-15 took place against a backdrop of increasing climate mobilization by non-state and sub-state actors as well as informal intergovernmental organizations, such as the Group of Eight (G8), Group of Twenty (G20) and the Major Economies Forum (MEF). Yet, despite this growing momentum outside the UNFCCC, parties were not able to bridge their differences at Copenhagen. With negotiations stalled in both the Kyoto track and the UNFCCC track, the summit saw a small group of heads of state hammer out a political agreement, known as the Copenhagen Accord, that would merely be noted, not adopted, by the COP plenary (Falkner, Stephan and Vogler, 2010).

At the time, COP-15 was widely perceived as a disaster, with some wondering whether it would 'spell the end of the UNFCCC process' (Yvo De Boer qtd. in Vidal, 2010). In hindsight, Copenhagen presented a significant turning point for the UNFCCC, prompting the rise of a more polycentric and flexible global climate change regime, built on a bottom-up logic (Bäckstrand and Lövbrand, 2016). In many ways, the Copenhagen Accords already included most of the core elements that would later be incorporated into the Paris Agreement, including: the 2°C target, a system of nationally determined pledges by all countries, a more flexible approach to differentiation, a shift towards transparency over legal enforcement, and recognition of the urgent need to mobilize climate finance from public and private sources (Bodansky, 2015). The post-Copenhagen period also saw notable developments beyond the formal UNFCCC negotiations. New forms of climate governance led by a diversity of actors made the landscape for global climate action much more diverse and multi-levelled (Jordan et al., 2015; Bäckstrand et al., 2017). Changing political conditions, most notably the willingness of the United States and China to collaborate on reducing GHG emissions (The White House, 2014), combined with the skilful orchestration by the French COP presidency, created a favourable environment for reaching an agreement at COP-21 in Paris.

4.2 The Paris Agreement: A New Framework for Global Climate Action

The adoption of the 2015 Paris Agreement has been widely celebrated as a 'monumental triumph' (United Nations, 2015) and a 'historic achievement' (European Commission, 2018: 3). It reflects a global consensus on the need for climate action by all countries to confine temperature rises to well below 2 ° C – and ideally 1.5 °C – above pre-industrial levels. Scholars have argued that the agreement enshrines a 'new logic' of global cooperation (Falkner, 2016a) which could provide 'a model for effective global governance in the twenty-first century' (Slaughter, 2015). From an international law perspective, the Agreement turns many long-held assumptions about what makes a successful treaty on their head. Whereas traditional international legal standards call for highly prescriptive binding commitments and a strong enforcement apparatus, the Paris Agreement embodies a flexible and facilitative approach. It creates a unique blend of hard, soft and non-law as well as bottom-up and top-down mechanisms (Rajamani, 2016a). Thus, the Paris Agreement represents a decisive shift away from the legalized regulatory logic of the Kyoto regime, enabling a more inclusive model of global climate governance. Key elements include:

Nationally determined rather than negotiated commitments: Rather than determining mitigation targets through multilateral negotiations, the Paris Agreement requires parties to determine their own nationally determined contributions (NDCs) and strengthen their efforts over time. Importantly, NDCs are submitted by every state party, making the Paris Agreement the first universal climate treaty. Unlike the national targets specified in the Kyoto Protocol, targets put forward in NDCs under the Paris Agreement are not legally binding. However, 'they are subject to binding procedural requirements and to normative expectations of progression and highest possible ambition' (Rajamani and Brunnée, 2017: 537).

Transparency rather than compliance mechanisms: Under the Kyoto Protocol, compliance with national mitigation targets was monitored by an independent committee, which also had the powers to impose sanctions for non-compliance, e.g. by suspending eligibility for flexibility mechanisms (Lefeber and Oberthür, 2012). In contrast, the Paris Agreement 'essentially substitutes transparency for compliance' (Slaughter, 2015). Under the Agreement's enhanced transparency framework, parties are required to submit biannual progress reports which are subject to technical expert reviews and a facilitative, multilateral peer review process. However, there are no sanctions for failing to meet nationally determined targets. The Agreement explicitly states that the enhanced transparency frame-work must be implemented 'in a facilitative, non-intrusive, non-punitive manner' that is 'respectful of national sovereignty' and avoids 'placing undue burden on Parties' (UNFCCC, 2015). Thus, the Agreement relies primarily on peer pressure and reputational costs as a way to ensure compliance.

A nuanced approach to differentiation: The Paris Agreement transcends the static division between Annex I and non-Annex I countries reflected in the Convention and the Kyoto Protocol. Yet, it does not abandon differentiation altogether. Rather, it applies 'differentiation along a much broader set of parameters, in a manner that allows for more diversity and dynamism, while building on the normative legacy of the Convention' (Voigt and Ferreira, 2016: 58). The Agreement qualifies the long-standing CBDR–RC principle by adding the phrase 'in the light of different national circumstances', a formulation first introduced at COP-20 in Lima. In addition, application of differentiation varies across the different elements of the Agreement. There are still references to 'developed' and 'developing' countries, with the former expected to take the lead on mitigation and provide technological and capacity-building support to the latter, however, these categories are not explicitly defined. This nuanced approach to differentiation was key to achieving an agreement that is both inclusive and ambitious (Rajamani, 2016b).

A cooperative approach to ambition raising: Although compliance with the Kyoto Protocol over the first commitment period was high (Grubb, 2016), the treaty did not deliver much in terms of total global emissions reductions. This was due to limited participation but also the fact that 'by setting a static emissions reduction target, the regime failed to create dynamic incentives to decarbonize the economy' (Falkner 2016a: 1110–11). The Paris Agreement seeks to avoid stagnation of climate ambition by establishing a five-yearly 'global stocktake' which assesses the collective progress towards achieving its long-term goals and opportunities to ratchet up ambition. Subsequently, all parties are required to submit new and strengthened NDCs that are informed by the outcome of the stocktake. A first 'test run' for the global stocktake was the Talanoa Dialogue, which was initiated at COP-23 in Bonn and concluded at COP-24 in Katowice with the 'Talanoa Call for Action' (UNFCCC, 2018).

A more prominent treatment of adaptation and loss and damage: Alongside the 2–1.5 °C mitigation goal, the Paris Agreement establishes a collective long-term goal 'of enhancing adaptive capacity, strengthening resilience and redu-cing vulnerability to climate change' (UNFCCC, 2015). All Parties are expected to facilitate, fund or undertake adaptation activities and report on them. However, progress towards the global adaptation goal is likely to be hindered by its ambiguity and the fact that the status of adaptation as a global public good remains contested (Persson, 2019). The Paris Agreement is also the first international climate treaty to 'recognize the importance of averting, minimizing and addressing loss and damage'; that is, climate impacts that go beyond adaptation (UNFCCC, 2015). However, the accompanying Paris Decision explicitly rules out the possibility of legal liability and compensation (UNFCCC, 2016).

Integration of transnational climate action into the UNFCCC regime: It is now widely recognized that non-state and sub-state actors (e.g. cities, regions, NGOs, businesses and investors) will play a crucial role in the implementation of the Paris Agreement, both by engaging in climate action themselves and by holding states to account if their efforts fall short. Under the regulatory Kyoto regime, non-state engagement with UNFCCC processes was limited. Since the 2009 Copenhagen Summit, however, the global climate regime has gradually moved towards a 'catalytic and facilitative' model that 'aims to bring cities and subnational governments, businesses, and other non-state actors into its very core' (Hale, 2016: 13). While non-state actors are not given much attention in the Paris Agreement itself, their contributions are recognized in the accompanying Paris Decision (UNFCCC, 2016). More significantly, since 2014, the UNFCCC has launched a number of orchestration efforts to galvanize and facilitate ambitious non-state action (Chan and Amling, 2019). The adoption of the Paris Agreement consolidated these efforts, cementing the shift towards what Bäckstrand et al. (2017) have termed 'hybrid multilateralism'.

Finance: The Paris Agreement also breaks new ground with regard to finance. For the first time, it sets a long-term goal to '[make] finance flows consistent with a pathway towards low greenhouse gas emissions and climate-resilient development' (UNFCCC, 2015). This provision goes beyond previous commitments to mobilize climate finance for mitigation and adaptation activities in developing countries, by calling for a fundamental shift of *all* financial flows, public and private, to support the transition to a low-carbon, climate-resilient economy. While the finance goal is qualitative in nature, it is clear that it is closely related to the other long-term goals on mitigation and adaptation and the 'pathways' they will generate (Rajamani and Werksman, 2018). In addition to the long-term finance goal, the Paris Agreement requires developed countries to continue to take the lead in providing financial support for mitigation and adaptation in developing countries. Other countries are encouraged to provide climate finance on a voluntary basis. The decision adopting the Paris Agreement also reconfirms the existing commitment of the international community to mobilize USD 100 billion of climate finance a year, with a new and higher collective goal to be set by 2025 (UNFCCC, 2016). While progress has been made, current efforts are still insufficient, with total climate finance for developing countries reaching only about USD 70 billion in 2017 (OECD, 2019).

4.3 Moving beyond Gridlock: Towards Implementation of the Paris Agreement

Reflecting strong political momentum, the Paris Agreement became one of the fastest multilateral agreements ever to enter into force. Over the course of just one year, the Agreement reached a sufficient number ratifications to take effect, shortly before COP-22 in Marrakech. Even the election of US president Donald Trump, who had made withdrawal from the treaty one of his campaign promises, did not diminish the resolve by other state parties to push ahead towards implementation. At COP-24 in Katowice, the Paris 'rulebook' was finalized, specifying rules, procedures and guidelines for the various elements of the Agreement. While parties were unable to agree on rules for voluntary cooperation and market mechanisms, overall, the rulebook turned out to be 'more robust than many had dared to expect' (Obergassel et al., 2019: 6).

Despite this progress, the Paris Agreement remains a 'promissory note' (Christoff, 2016). Aggregate national pledges made thus far are insufficient for keeping global warming below 2 °C, let alone 1.5 °C (Climate Action Tracker, 2019). The Agreement's success thus hinges on whether ambition will be scaled up significantly over time and whether pledges will be fully implemented. Recent developments have not instilled much confidence that progress is being made towards achieving the long-term mitigation goal of the Paris Agreement, especially in light of US withdrawal which was formalized on 4 November 2019 (US Department of State, 2019). In the eyes of some observers, COP-24 'clearly failed in its task to urgently call on Parties to increase their mitigation ambition' (Obergassel et al., 2019: 8). While the Talanoa Dialogue – the first trial run for the Agreement's ambition mechanism – produced a 'Call for Action' that emphasized the need to act 'with urgency' (UNFCCC, 2018), the COP decision failed to reflect this urgency, merely 'inviting' parties to 'consider' the Dialogue's outcomes (Verkuijl and van Asselt, 2019: 17). In addition, the refusal of four oil- and gas-producing countries – the United States, Saudi Arabia, Russia and Kuwait – to 'welcome' the IPCC's special report on global warming of 1.5 °C at Katowice raised fears that an anti-climate science coalition led by the United States might attempt to actively undermine future global collaborative action (Watts and Doherty, 2018).

Ominous signs of backtracking continued to be on display at COP-25 held in Madrid in December 2019, with UN Secretary-General António Guterres 'disappointed' with the results of what was meant to be an opportunity to show increased ambition (UNFCCC, 2019a). Two weeks of fraught negotiation made little headway on several key issues, including Article 6 (global carbon market mechanisms), NDC timeframes and adaptation financing. A proposed 'status report' on whether promised financial transfers of USD 100 billion by 2020 had been delivered was predictably opposed by developed country parties (HSBC, 2019). The issue of finance is closely related to L&D, with no progress made on the WIM and the United States successful in ensuring that the WIM remains outside the COP process (Timperley, 2019). Echoing the reticence at COP-24 to endorse the science, the two special reports on 'Climate Change and Land' and 'Oceans and Cryosphere' released by the IPCC in 2019 were 'noted', but not 'welcomed', by COP-25 delegates. The outcome text was also heavily criticized for failing to protect people on the ground from harm caused by activities under the proposed new market mechanisms (CIEL, 2019).

COP-25 was meant to focus on boosting post-2020 ambition. The disappointing outcome means that COP-26 to be held in Glasgow, Scotland, in early 2021 (postponed due to COVID-19) is now likely to become high stakes for the entire UNFCCC process. However, raising ambition and breaking the deadlock on a series of post-Paris controversies will be especially difficult in light of the COVID-19 crisis and with UK diplomats and civil service already burdened by the UK's withdrawal from the EU. While the pandemic is causing a temporary drop in global GHG emissions, it is unclear whether it will help or hinder making the long-term structural changes required to decarbonize the economy (Norton, 2020). In addition, COVID-19 poses challenges to street-based climate activism (Fahys, 2020) and even climate science (Berwyn, 2020). The Paris Agreement alone was never going to halt global climate change. Much now depends on whether national-level policies, institutions and mechanisms are able to connect the Paris Agreement's provisions to local realities. However, interstate consensus seems to be in short supply and time is running out. Importantly, as the next section surveys, the implementation of global climate policy does not begin and end with formal intergovernmental organizations. Indeed, the Paris Agreement is opening up new opportunities for climate mobilization by diverse actors, including a globalizing climate movement. Organizations like Extinction Rebellion and the climate activist Greta Thunberg, named TIME's Person of the Year 2019, are pioneering radical forms of climate action in an effort to sound the alarm. 2021 may well prove to be a defining moment for a UNFCCC process which many in the global climate movement believe is unwilling or unable to close the yawning gap between current progress and global goals on mitigation and adaptation.

5 Mapping of Actors Involved in Global Climate Change Governance

An extensive scholarship has documented the huge diversity of actors engaged in global climate change governance (Betsill and Bulkeley, 2006; Bäckstrand, 2008; Pattberg and Stripple, 2008; Hoffmann, 2011; Green, 2014). This section identifies which are the main actors operating in this governance domain and examines to what extent they have the capability (and authority) to initiate policy initiatives, and foster coordination among multiple actors in pursuing agreed objectives. It proceeds by differentiating between formal and informal international organizations, followed by a structured breakdown of actors by levels of analysis (e.g. international, regional, local), as well as by sector (e.g. public, private, hybrid).

5.1 Formal International Organizations

The main interstate multilateral organizations operating in the global climate change domain include the UNFCCC, the IPCC and UN Environment, which coordinates the UN's environmental activities. Additional relevant intergovernmental organizations are also identified, reflecting the fact that climate change impacts almost all aspects of international cooperation.

5.1.1 United Nations Framework Convention on Climate Change (UNFCCC)

The UNFCCC is the foundational treaty of the international climate regime, defining its core objectives, principles, rules and procedures. At the same time, the UNFCCC is also a formal intergovernmental organization with a sophisticated institutional and administrative infrastructure to support treaty implementation, monitor progress and enable the negotiation of new legal instruments under the Convention. Its supreme decision-making body, the Conference of the Parties (COP), includes all states that have ratified the Convention and it meets annually to review and assess implementation of the treaty. Since the UNFCCC entered into force, the COP has negotiated two separate instruments to complement the Convention: the Kyoto Protocol (whose second commitment period will end in 2020) and the Paris Agreement (which covers the period from 2020 onward). Together, they form the legal and institutional foundation of the global climate change regime, supplemented by COP decisions which specify technical details and procedural rules.

Although closely related, the Convention, the Kyoto Protocol and the Paris Agreement 'are separate treaties, with overlapping but distinct membership'

(Bodansky, Brunnée and Rajamani, 2017: 87). The implementation of the Kyoto Protocol and the Paris Agreement is overseen by the Conference of the Parties serving as the meeting of the Parties to the Kyoto Protocol (CMP) and the Conference of the Parties serving as the meeting of the Parties to the Paris Agreement (CMA). The CMP and the CMA convene each year during the same period as the COP. During meetings of the CMP or the CMA, parties that have not ratified these instruments are allowed to participate as observers but do not have the right to take decisions. The default mode of decision-making in the COP, CMP and CMA is consensus, often noted as a major obstacle for more progressive action as 'a single country can potentially stall the entire process' (Hale, 2017: 189).

The COP, CMP and CMA are supported by a permanent secretariat based in Bonn and two subsidiary bodies established under the Convention: the Subsidiary Body for Scientific and Technological Advice (SBSTA) and the Subsidiary Body for Implementation (SBI). The Convention also provides for a financial mechanism as well as a 'comparatively strong implementation machinery' (Bodansky, Brunnée and Rajamani, 2017: 104). Under this core institutional infrastructure (see Figure 1), a dense web of working groups, committees and programs has developed to govern different elements of the regime (Pattberg and Widerberg, 2017).

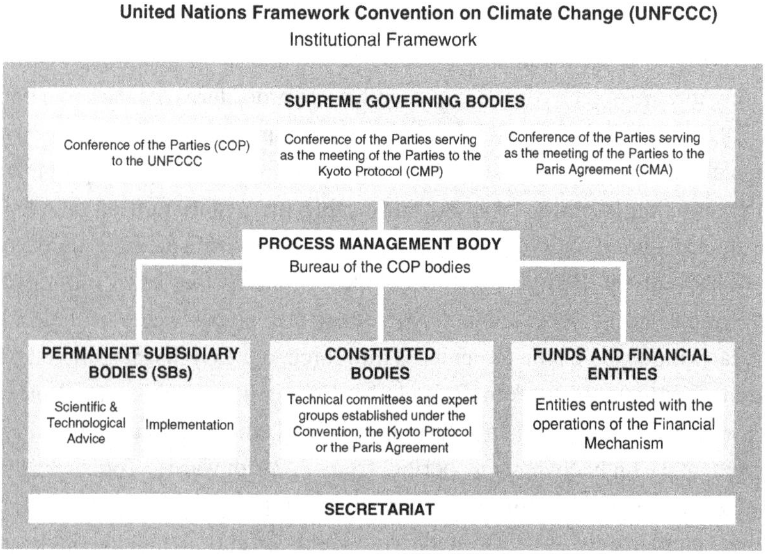

Figure 1 UNFCCC institutional framework

Source: based on information obtained from UNFCCC

Key challenges facing the UNFCCC include clarifying its mandate, independence and powers of the secretariat, resource constraints and the absence of enforcement mechanisms.

Clarifying its mandate. The UNFCCC's mandate was originally quite vague, with Article 2 of the Convention not providing any specific targets or timetables (United Nations, 1992). The 2015 Paris Agreement has delivered a political interpretation of what is needed to prevent 'dangerous' climate change, by enshrining a collective global target of keeping global warming to well below 2 °C and ideally 1.5 °C. Thus, with regard to mitigation, the UNFCCC now has a precise and measurable mandate.

However, there is widespread agreement that '[t]he UNFCCC process has not been effective (enough) in catalyzing mitigation action compatible with a below-2°C trajectory' (Hermwille et al., 2017: 151). What is more, the 2 °C target itself is widely considered insufficient to prevent some of the worst impacts of climate change. Partly as a result of the slow progress on mitigation, adaptation and loss and damage (L&D) have become increasingly important components of the UNFCCC's mandate. For the first time, the Paris Agreement establishes a long-term global goal on adaptation, although key challenges remain with regard to its operationalization, given 'the relative fuzziness of adaptation as a policy area' (Lesnikowski et al., 2017: 827). Even harder will be the establishment and evaluation of concrete coordinated responses to L&D under the Paris Agreement.

Independence and powers of the secretariat. The independence, powers and political influence of the UNFCCC bureaucracy have traditionally been considered limited. All legal and political decision makers' powers lie with the COP, CMP and CMA. The secretariat has no regulatory competencies, enforcement powers or scientific research tasks. It serves primarily as an information hub, technical advisor and negotiation facilitator. As Busch (2009: 254) argues, this narrow mandate is partly a reflection of the politically sensitive nature of the climate change regime as 'most parties do not want a strong and independent climate secretariat'. Therefore, the UNFCCC bureaucracy has not been viewed as instrumental in shaping political decisions, although Yamin and Depledge (2004: 507) note that the strategic advice provided by the secretariat 'can be absolutely crucial in steering the negotiations towards a successful outcome'.

Green (2010) argues that the relative weakness of the UNFCCC secretariat has also contributed to the proliferation of private regulations in areas such as corporate-level GHG accounting. The secretariat was involved in the early work of the Clean Development Mechanism (CDM) which, in 2005, became the first global exchange for carbon offsets, allowing countries to receive credit for financing emissions-reduction activities outside their borders (Green, 2017). Yet, it was never feasible that the poorly resourced secretariat would take on the monitoring and verification responsibilities under the CDM (Green, 2010: 118). However, there are signs that the role of the UNFCCC secretariat is changing as the regime as a whole is undergoing a profound transformation. Hickmann et al. (2019: 2) argue that the UNFCCC secretariat 'has gradually loosened its straitjacket and expanded its original spectrum of activity by engaging different sub-national and non-state actors into a policy dialogue using facilitative orchestration as a mode of governance'.

Resource constraints. The UNFCCC has a proposed core budget for 2020–21 of USD 75.7 million (UNFCCC, 2019b). This represents a tiny fraction of the overall UN program budget of USD 2.87 billion for 2020 proposed by the UN Secretary-General for 2020–21 (Lebada, 2019). UNFCCC funding has been impacted by the system-wide decrease of US financial support for international cooperation on climate change (Zhang et al., 2017). It is important to note also that the UNFCCC cannot deploy financial resources for implementation of policy delivery programs. Program funding is provided by the Global Environmental Facility (GEF) which operates outside the UNFCCC and is not supervised by any single international organization. The GEF is governed through its own intergovernmental bodies and enlists diverse international organizations, such as UN Development Programme (UNDP), UN Environment and the World Bank, as 'implementing agencies', which coordinate applications for funding and managing GEF funded projects in-house. Graham and Thompson (2015), in analyzing this unusual arrangement, demonstrate how state interests have served to limit GEF capabilities, leading the body to rely upon orchestration of third-party organizations. However, they also highlight the potentially positive development of new entrants into the climate funding ecosystem, including the Adaptation Fund, established by the parties to the Kyoto Protocol (Adaptation Fund, n.d.), and a new Green Climate Fund established as a second 'operating entity' of the UNFCCC's financial mechanism, in addition to the GEF (Green Climate Fund, n.d.).

Absence of enforcement mechanisms. It is likely that some kind of global enforcement will be a necessary addition to the voluntary arrangement established by the Paris Agreement. As Harari (2017) reflects, 'I think the imperative of having some kind of real ability to force through difficult decisions at the global level is more important than almost anything else'. However, there is currently no effective hierarchy at the global scale capable of delivering costs to individuals who are moved to violate the collective interest. Reflecting this systemic reality, the Paris Agreement is premised on interstate cooperation, explicitly committing itself to functioning in a 'transparent, non-adversarial, non-punitive manner' (UNFCCC, 2015). This is a significant departure from earlier controversial efforts to enforce compliance in the climate regime, especially under the Kyoto Protocol (Brunnée, Doelle and Rajamani, 2011). Voluntary peer review mechanisms operating within the UNFCCC, such as the international technical expert review of state parties' emission target performance, offer the promise of enforcing collective discipline through strategic relationships (Terman and Voeten, 2018). However, Gollier and Tirole (2015: 5) argue that the ambitious mitigation required by 2030 can only be achieved through enforcement schemes 'based on financial and trade penalties to induce all countries to participate and comply with the agreement'.

5.1.2 Intergovernmental Panel on Climate Change (IPCC)

The IPCC was established in 1988 by the World Meteorological Organization (WMO) and the United Nations Environment Programme (UNEP) to provide the international community with scientific guidance on the magnitude and temporal progression of climate change, its potential impact and the range of realistic response strategies (UNGA, 1988). It is best known for its five Assessment Reports (with the sixth report due to be released in 2021). The IPCC currently has 195 member states which meet at least once a year in a plenary session of the Panel, which is the ultimate decision-making body of the IPCC. The Panel operates by consensus to set the IPCC's structures, procedures, budgets and work programs, to approve and adopt its reports, and to elect the IPCC chair and other members of the Bureau for the duration of an assessment cycle. The Bureau consists of thirty-four expert members and provides advice to the Panel, as well as overseeing the Working Groups (WGs) that produce the IPCC's assessment reports.

There are three WGs, each of which is responsible for one volume of the assessment reports: WG-I focuses on the physical science behind climate change, WG-II assesses climate change vulnerability and options for adaptation, and WG-III focusses on strategies for climate change mitigation. Each WG receives administrative support from a technical support unit; the overall Bureau is supported by a small secretariat based in Geneva. There is also a Task Force on National Greenhouse Gas Inventories which develops internationally agreed methodologies and guidelines for calculating and reporting national greenhouse gas emissions and removals. It has its own Task Force Bureau, which is also elected by the Panel during plenary sessions.

Key challenges facing the IPCC include close supervision by interstate hierarchies, the political challenge of communicating scientific uncertainty, misinformation campaigns by powerful vested interests, and legitimacy deficits.

Reports require approval by interstate hierarchy. The role of the IPCC is purely advisory and not focused on producing original science. Rather than undertaking independent scientific research, the IPCC reviews and synthesizes the latest climate research in an effort to build international consensus among both scientists and governments. Its reports aim to be 'neutral, policy-relevant but not policy-prescriptive' (IPCC, n.d.). From the very beginning, the IPCC has played the hybrid role of a 'boundary organization', enhancing cooperation between scientists and policy makers but seeking to maintain a distinct boundary between these two worlds (Hulme, 2009). While its reports are drafted by thousands of scientists and experts around the world, the IPCC remains an explicitly intergovernmental organization and its outputs require approval from governments. Thus, the IPCC has the difficult task of developing consensus knowledge that is both 'scientifically sound and politically acceptable' (Agrawala, 1998: 621).

The complexity of assessing biosphere stability is fraught with scientific uncertainty. The IPCC's work has often been laden by controversy. The need to issue credible and legitimate consensus statements for a wide range of audiences on a topic characterized by fundamental uncertainty makes the work of the IPCC inherently thorny. Policymakers have turned expert input on the uncertainties of climate change into a quantifiable fact: a dangerous 2 °C limit (Shaw, 2017). However, as climate scientists readily admit, the central concern is not absolute change in one climatic measure, but multiple 'known' and 'unknown' tipping points which threaten to make any effort at predictive modelling obsolete (Lenton et al., 2008). As a boundary organization operating across science, policy and public discourse, the IPCC must face the ongoing challenge of avoiding an over-politicization of science as well as an over-scientization of politics (Hoppe, Wesselink and Cairns, 2013). Some have concluded that the IPCC set up as an intergovernmental organization is fundamentally flawed, so that '[t]he degree to which the IPCC is capable of generating usable knowledge is largely politically circumscribed' (Haas and Stevens, 2011: 145).

Misinformation campaigns targeting the IPCC. The IPCC has also faced attacks on its scientific credibility, in particular in light of the 2009 'climategate', which was triggered by the hack of emails by scientists involved in its work, and the subsequent exposure of mistakes in the Fourth Assessment Report (Carrington, 2011). In response, the IPCC introduced various initiatives to improve public accountability and transparency, including through an external review and an overhaul of its communication strategy, although these efforts have been criticized as narrow and insufficient (Beck, 2012). As Beck and Mahony (2018: 11) argue, the recent emergence of so-called 'post-truth' politics may pose a significant new challenge to the IPCC, which could 'become the lightning rod to an increasingly partisan politics in a highly politicized public context, especially in the United States and United Kingdom'. However, the IPCC has long been a priority target of fossil fuel lobby groups intent on manipulating UN climate negotiations (Savage and Hope, 2019). Such activity takes place against a backdrop of massive lobbying by fossil fuel groups of the EU and other key intergovernmental organizations (CEO, 2019).

Legitimacy deficits. Trust in the work of the IPCC is also negatively affected by the underrepresentation of scholars from the Global South (Ho-Lem, Zerriffi and Kandlikar, 2011) and the dominance of scholars from specific disciplines (Corbera et al., 2016). The IPCC has sought to diversify its geographical and disciplinary make-up, although significant biases remain with important consequences for the credibility, legitimacy and policy relevance of its assessments (Berg and Lidskog, 2018). Finally, going forward, the IPCC is also facing the practical challenge of dealing with the sheer magnitude of new climate research in a comprehensive and transparent fashion (Minx et al., 2017).

5.1.3 UN Environment (Formerly UNEP)

The United Nations Environment Programme (UNEP) was established by the General Assembly in 1972, shortly after the first high-level Conference on the Human Environment in Stockholm. Since its inception, UNEP's mandate has been amended and strengthened several times but at its core has always been to ensure collaboration and coordination of environmental action within the UN system. It also provides specialist knowledge and policy guidance for such action and it contributes to the development of international environmental law. UNEP administers several multilateral environmental agreements (MEAs), including the Convention on Biological Diversity as well as the Vienna Convention and its Montreal Protocol on Substances that Deplete the Ozone Layer.

It played a key role in negotiating the UNFCCC, however, it has subsequently become somewhat marginalized from the climate change discussion as the UNFCCC Secretariat has assumed a more prominent policy coordination function (Drexhage, 2008). That said, it continues to produce the authoritative Emissions Gap Reports. These reports are prepared by an international team of leading scientists and seek to identify policy pathways to bridge existing emissions gaps and the latest scientific information, including the IPCC Special Report on 1.5 °C (UNEP, 2018). Headquartered in Nairobi, UNEP might be able to better reflect the views, needs and priorities of the Global South with regard to climate action. However, 'UNEP's location away from the centers of political activity [has] hampered its ability to coordinate the specialized agency, to assert itself as the central actor in global environmental, and to attract and retain the most highly-qualified policy staff' (Ivanova, 2008: 161).

UNEP 'is by almost all accounts not up to the task of managing the response to climate change. UNEP suffers from a vague mandate, severe budget constraints, limited analytical capacity, and other human resource challenges as well as a lack of political support' (Esty, 2009: 427).

The decision to constitute UNEP as a Subsidiary Programme to the UN General Assembly rather than a more autonomous and empowered specialized agency, such as the World Health Organization, has arguably impacted its authority (Ivanova, 2005). Efforts by the EU and African Union to upgrade UNEP into a UN Environment Organization or a World Environment Organization have been repeatedly thwarted by opposition from the United States and other state parties. The agency was identified in the 2012 Rio+20 outcome document as the 'leading global environmental authority that sets the global environmental agenda' (United Nations, 2012: 23). However, the reality belies the lofty rhetoric. Efforts have been made to strengthen UNEP in recent years, including by providing for universal membership and more secure, stable and increased financial resources in 2012 (UNEP, 2012). However, UNEP continues to lack the political, financial, legal and operational resources which would be commensurate with its mandate to be 'the leading global environmental authority'.

As the main environmental coordinating body of the UN, UNEP could play an important coordinating function and catalytic role in ensuring that climate change action is integrated throughout the UN. However, this function is undermined by low policy focality in a densely populated regime ecosystem, chronic underfunding and repeated problematic appointments to senior leadership positions (Berglund, 2018). Van der Lugt and Dingwerth (2015) attribute the limited capabilities displayed by UNEP largely to divergent interests among state parties, especially when it comes to oversight of private sector activities by the Paris-based UNEP Division on Technology, Industry and Economics (UNEP DTIE) and its Geneva-based UNEP FI Secretariat.

5.1.4 Other Intergovernmental Organizations

The problem of climate change cuts through many other issues of international cooperation. Therefore, '[a]cross the United Nations, virtually all of the various programs, agencies, and affiliates have wrestled with how to address climate change as part of their work' (Conca, 2018: 4). This is also true for many intergovernmental organizations (IGOs) operating outside the UN system. UN-related IGOs that engage in (or collaborate on) climate change related action include:

- **Other environmental institutions within the UN**, such as the Global Environment Facility (GEF), which is the financial mechanism for the major international environmental conventions, and the ozone regime under the Vienna Convention for the protection of the Ozone Layer.
- **UN principal organs**, including the General Assembly, the Security Council, the Economic and Social Council, and the Secretariat, **as well as their subsidiary bodies and high-level policy fora**, such as the Human Rights Council, the UN High-level Political Forum on Sustainable Development (HLPF) or the UN Forum on Forests.
- **Specialized UN agencies**, such as the Food and Agriculture Organization (FAO), the World Meteorological Organization (WMO), the World Health Organization (WHO), the World Food Programme (WFP), the World Bank, the International Monetary Fund (IMF), the International Labour Organization (ILO), the UN Educational, Scientific and Cultural Organization (UNESCO), the International Civil Aviation Organization (ICAO) and the International Maritime Organization (IMO).
- **UN programs and funds,** such as the UN Development Programme (UNDP), the UN Refugee Agency (UNHCR), the UN Population Fund (UNFPA), the UN Children's Fund (UNICEF) and the UN Human Settlements Programme (UN-Habitat).
- **UN departments and offices,** such as the UN Office for Disaster Risk Reduction (UNISDR) or the Office of the UN High Commissioner for Human Rights (OHCHR).
- **Related organizations**, such as the World Trade Organization (WTO).

There are many opportunities for partnerships, collaboration and synergies between IGOs engaging with the problem of climate change. Focal actors for particular issues and sectors, such as the IMO and ICAO, could play an important coordinating function in their own right (Smith and Tanveer, 2018). However, there is also a need to address potential conflict where the change regime intersects with other policy regimes. 'Such concerns have emerged particularly in the context of the World Trade Organization (WTO), with climate policymakers becoming apprehensive that WTO law could limit the ways in which they can implement effective domestic climate policies. At the same time, there are concerns that trade-related climate measures could be used for protectionist purposes' (Das et al., 2018: 6).

5.2 Informal Intergovernmental Organizations

The past few decades have seen a marked shift from formal, legalized governance arrangements to more informal modes of international cooperation. This is reflected, inter alia, in the growing number of informal intergovernmental organizations (IIGOs) (Roger, 2020). Whereas formal intergovernmental organizations (IGOs) are 'official interstate arrangements legalized through a charter or international treaty, and coordinated by a permanent secretariat, staff, or headquarters', IIGOs do not operate through legally binding agreements and they do not have sophisticated bureaucratic structures (Vabulas and Snidal, 2013: 194). Nevertheless, they meet on a regular basis and they have explicitly defined goals, consistent practices and a relatively permanent membership, which 'occurs on the state level between Heads of Government and State, Ambassadors, and high-level Ministers' (Vabulas, 2019: 404). This differentiates IIGOs from purely ad hoc arrangements of policy coordination as well as other informal actors, such as transnational public–private governance initiatives. Prominent examples of IIGOs explored in this section include the various G-Groups (in particular the G7/8 and G20), which first emerged in the field of international financial and economic governance, as well as the more recent Major Economies Forum (MEF).

After the failure of the 2009 Copenhagen summit to produce a new climate treaty, some analysts suggested that IIGOs may offer a more realistic tool for responding to climate change than the cumbersome UNFCCC negotiation process (Keohane and Victor, 2011). As Falkner (2016b: 87) notes, such 'minilateral' solutions 'promise more effective bargaining among the main climate powers, better incentives to encourage mitigation efforts and discourage free-riding, and new ways to align international power asymmetries with the interests of the global climate regime.' However, he cautions that informal clubs do not offer a panacea to the climate crisis, as they 'cannot pressurize or induce reluctant great powers to reduce their greenhouse gas emissions' (Falkner, 2016b: 97).

Others have been more critical of the growing importance of climate change IIGOs, arguing that they promote 'forum shopping' and may 'undermine a universal approach within the UN system' (Vogler, 2018: 26). While it may be easier to find consensus in informal 'great power clubs', these groups raise a number of questions regarding legitimacy, representation, transparency and accountability. Climate change will affect the poorest communities first and most severely, however, their views and needs are underrepresented in most IIGOs. Finally, the informal character and restricted membership may make IIGOs particularly vulnerable to political changes in key member states. A case in point is the collapse of the MEF under the Trump administration and recent US attempts to take climate change off the G7 agenda (Holden, 2019).

5.2.1 From the G7/8 to the G20

The G7 (known as the G8 between 1997 and 2014 when Russia was a member) first emerged in 1975 as a regular informal platform for exchange and cooperation among industrialized states. Originally conceived as a forum for economic cooperation, the G7 gradually expanded its agenda to include a diversity of issues, from health to security (Larionova and Kirton, 2015). Forty years ago, G7 leaders first explicitly linked the development of alternative energy sources with the need to control carbon dioxide emissions in the atmosphere, thus putting climate change on the group's agenda (G7 Information Centre, n.d.). Since 1985, the G7/8 has generated a substantial number of 'specific, measurable, future-oriented collective decisional commitments' on climate change (Kirton and Guebert, 2009: 1). It was thus the first global governance institution to produce concrete responses to the climate change challenge, long before the UN took up the issue (Kirton and Kokotsis, 2015).

However, the G7/8's 'global climate leadership has been neither continuous nor comprehensive in covering all component issues contained within, or related to, climate change control' (Kokotsis, 2017: 90). Assessments of the G7/8's performance with regard to climate change governance have also varied widely. While some have argued that the G7/G8's neo-liberalist agenda may be fundamentally incompatible with environmental sustainability (Gill, 2012), others have suggested that the G7/8 'has been more effective than its UN counterpart as a center of global climate governance' (Kirton and Guebert, 2009: 2).

More recently, the leadership role of the G7/8 has declined in relative terms. When the G7/8 member countries first made concrete commitments on climate change, they were responsible for the vast majority of global GHG emissions. By 2012, they accounted for less than a quarter of GHG emissions (Livingston, 2016). As a result, 'climate change had become a joint venture of both the G8 and G20' (Kokotsis, 2017: 85). Many regard the G20 as a more promising and inclusive venue, able to bridge long-standing differences between the Global North and the Global South and navigate boundary conflicts between trade, environment and development issues (Johnson, 2001). The G20 Presidency of Saudi Arabia in 2020 has announced 'safeguarding the planet' as one of its priorities, with a focus on managing emissions, combating land degradation and habitant loss, preserving the oceans, as well as fostering financing and innovation to tackle water insecurity and other public goods (G20, 2019). However, the G20 is yet to take a lead in tackling climate change. Although the G20's 2009 Pittsburgh Summit promised to phase out all fossil fuel subsidies by 2025, G20 countries still provide USD 150 billion annually for exploration and extraction of fossil fuels for energy (Merrill and Funke, 2019). EU governments alone provided EUR 55 billion per year in fossil fuel subsidies in 2016 (Rademaekers et al., 2019: 265).

5.2.2 From the Major Economies Forum (MEF) to the Ministerial on Climate Action

The Major Economies Forum on Energy and Climate (MEF) was launched in 2009 by US President Barack Obama. It grew out of an earlier initiative by the Bush administration, the Major Emitters Forum. The MEF included sixteen countries and the European Union, together accounting for more than 80 per cent of global GHG emissions (van Asselt, 2014). Membership of the MEF overlapped significantly with the G20, however, its mandate exclusively covered climate change. The MEF primarily focused on facilitating candid high-level political discussions to create momentum for the UNFCCC process. It was instrumental in endorsing the 2 °C global temperature target in the run-up to the 2009 Copenhagen conference (Jaeger and Jaeger, 2011) and also played a key role in laying the groundwork for the Paris Agreement (Fehl and Thimm, 2019). Once considered the 'best candidate' for an IIGO response to climate change (Victor, 2009: 343), the MEF has been largely inactive under the Trump presidency. Since 2017, the EU, Canada and China have convened the Ministerial on Climate Action to replace the MEF, which brings together a group of thirty-four governments (Fehl and Thimm, 2019).

5.3 Regional Intergovernmental Organizations

Regional international organizations have an important role in enabling global climate policy implementation in local settings, enjoying three potential advantages: small number of actors, opportunities for issue-linkage, and linkage between national and global governance systems (Betsill, 2007). Well placed to navigate regional political, institutional and social settings, regional IGOs such as the African Union (AU), the Association of Southeast Asian Nations (ASEAN), the European Union (EU), and the Inter-American Institute for Global Change Research (IAI), have the potential to serve a vital 'metagovernance' function, elaborating regional-specific principles, rules and procedures, in alignment with UNFCCC standards (Sørensen and Torfing, 2009). Given space constraints, we focus on the EU, where institutionalized metagovernance is most advanced.

5.3.1 The European Union (EU)

The EU is widely considered a global leader in climate governance. According to its own assessment, it has 'the most advanced climate, energy and environmental legislation in the world' (European Commission, 2019: 7). The EU's long-term strategic vision, adopted in November 2018, calls for a climate-neutral economy by 2050 (European Commission, n.d.a). This was reinforced with the release of the initial framework for a European Green Deal by the Commission president in December 2019 (European Commission, n.d.b). In addition, the EU has adopted specific climate and energy targets for 2020 and 2030. Under its 2030 climate and energy framework, the EU commits to cutting GHG emissions by at least 40 per cent from 1990 levels, a target that is also reflected in its current nationally determined contribution (NDC) under the Paris Agreement. However, over the past decade, observers have diagnosed a decrease of EU ambition and innovation. This is partly due to external circumstances, specifically the period of uncertainty following the 2009 Copenhagen climate negotiations. More directly, it is a result of internal challenges, including the post-2008 recession (Skovgaard, 2014) and the shaky state of the wider European integration project (Zito, Burns and Lenschow, 2019). With deepening divisions between climate 'leaders' and 'laggards' in the EU, the recently unveiled European Green Deal is predicted 'to turn into a bruising political battle' (Tamma et al., 2019). Brexit is also likely to negatively affect EU climate ambition and weaken its position in UNFCCC negotiations (Bocse, 2019).

In the area of climate change – as in other policy areas – decision-making powers in the EU are divided among a variety of actors. An important focal actor within EU structures is the Environment Council, a configuration of the EU Council. It is composed of environment ministers from all EU Member States who usually meet four times a year. It is responsible, together with the European Parliament, for the adoption of most day-to-day environmental policy measures. It also responsible for preparing common EU positions for international climate change negotiations (Council of the European Union, n. d.). It is thus, 'the single most important actor shaping EU external climate policy' (Oberthür, 2011: 671). However, the European Commission is the only body that can propose EU legislation. Climate change falls under the responsibility of the Directorate-General for Climate Action or DG CLIMA, supported by a host of other relevant Directorate-Generals (European Commission, n.d.c). In the past, the European Commission has often provided significant entrepreneurship on climate change, from the establishment of the EU's Emissions Trading System (EU ETS) to the crafting of the first climate and energy package (Skjærseth, 2017). More recently, the scope for transformational climate leadership by the Commission has been constrained by internal divisions and a lack of support from member states, although the announced Green Deal indicates renewed commitment in this area.

European climate policy has accumulated over decades. The EU was an early mover, voluntarily committing to GHG emissions reduction efforts as early as 1990. It subsequently played a key role in the development of the global climate change regime and the adoption and entry into force of both the Kyoto Protocol and the Paris Agreement. The EU has consistently sought to establish itself as an ambitious and proactive actor, both in terms of influencing international negotiations and in terms of implementing exemplary climate policies (Van Schaik and Schunz, 2012). Today, many scholars would concur that the EU's internal and external climate policy ambitions have been an important instrument for European identity building, helping to generate support for the wider European project (Wurzel, Liefferink and Di Lullo, 2019). The EU's climate governance toolbox has traditionally relied on top-down regulatory instruments and accountability relationships, with the notable exception of the market-based EU ETS. However, recent reforms embody a shift towards a more bottom-up approach to EU climate and energy governance, based on integrated National Energy and Climate Plans (European Commission, n.d.d).

Overall, most observers agree that EU climate policy has been comparatively ambitious and successful. 'The EU has succeeded in decoupling its emissions from economic growth. Since 1990 GDP increased by 45% (to 2013) while emissions decreased by 19%. At the same time the obligations under the Kyoto Protocol to 2012 were achieved and surpassed: a reduction of 8% was promised; a reduction of 18% was delivered' (Delbeke and Vis, 2016). Qualifying claims of success, more critical perspectives emphasize that EU over-delivery on the Kyoto targets has been enabled by 'creative accounting' (Voosen, 2009) and developments that are unrelated to EU climate policy, including the 2008 economic crisis, which triggered a significant temporary drop in emissions. In addition, interest divergence across an expanded EU membership has meant that 'common political will for ambitious climate policy has become scarcer' (Rayner and Jordan, 2016). The 2030 EU climate and energy framework falls short of the EU's long-term ambition, which is itself insufficient to meet its commitments under the Paris Agreement (Climate Action Tracker, n.d.).

Notwithstanding, as the following case study highlights, the EU plays a key role in downloading UNFCCC requirements to enable regional compliance. It will be interesting to see whether the sophisticated monitoring, reporting and verification (MRV) system developed by the EU will serve as an exemplar for policy emulation across other regional settings (see Section 6.2.1 for further information on the MRV system under the Paris Agreement).

Case Study: EU Coordination of Greenhouse Gas Inventories

Inventories of GHG emissions and removals are an essential part of the UNFCCC-endorsed MRV system. Reliable information on national emission levels and trends are fundamental to defining appropriate mitigation targets and policies, tracking progress made and holding governments to account. EU member states report GHG inventories and related information to the Directorate General Climate Action (DG Climate Action) of the European Commission, the UNFCCC and UNECE.[3] National inventories are prepared in line with UNFCCC reporting requirements as well as the EU's Climate Monitoring Mechanism Regulation.[4] Internationally agreed methodologies to estimate and report GHG emissions and removals are laid out in the 2006 IPCC Guidelines for National Greenhouse Gas Inventories, which were last refined in 2019 (IPCC-TFI, n.d.).

Most EU countries prepared their first national inventories in the early 1990s and national institutional arrangements were broadly consolidated by the time the Kyoto Protocol entered into force. A preliminary review reveals a varied landscape of national institutional arrangements for GHG inventories in the EU.[5] Member states' national inventories provide the basis for compiling the GHG inventory for the EU as a whole. At the beginning of each year, the designated national 'single national entities' submit their inventories to DG Climate Action, which has overall responsibility for preparing, reporting and archiving the EU inventory (see Figure 2). The actual compilation of the inventory is led by the European Environment Agency (EEA), in collaboration with Eurostat and the Joint Research Centre (JRC). During this process, quality assurance and quality control checks are performed, thus providing an additional mechanism to ensure that member states' inventories are complete, correct and consistent. Implementation of the Paris Agreement opens up opportunities to further develop and review good practices for legal, procedural and institutional arrangements at the regional level.

---

[3] All EU member states have ratified the 1979 Geneva Convention on Long-Range Transboundary Air Pollution (LRTAP), negotiated under the auspices of the United Nations Economic Commission for Europe (UNECE).

[4] In 2021, the Climate Monitoring Mechanism Regulation will be replaced by the Regulation on the Governance of the Energy Union and Climate Action, which bring the EU's reporting mechanisms in line with the Paris Agreement (European Commission, n.d.e).

[5] The review is based on member states' 2019 national inventory submissions to the UNFCCC, all of which were found at https://unfccc.int/process-and-meetings/transparency-and-reporting /reporting-and-review-under-the-convention/greenhouse-gas-inventories-annex-i-parties/ national-inventory-submissions-2019

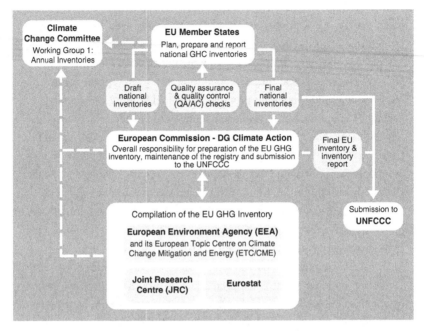

Figure 2 GHG emission inventory system of the EU

Source: based on information obtained from European Environment Agency (2019).

5.3.2 Other Regional Organizations

As with international institutions, the role of regional intergovernmental organizations in climate policy needs to be placed in the context of the broader structures in which they are embedded. Significant differences underpin the development of regional systems. The EU displays an exceptionally deep and complex institutionalization of climate policy, not emulated in any other regional regime. Regional variance partly reflects the extent of the embedding of climate policy norms within domestic political systems across regions. Multiple factors, from democratization to civil society activism to economic development, also shape the depth and breadth of regional climate institutionalization.

It is beyond the scope of this Element to engage in an in-depth analysis of regional developments in climate policy implementation. However, Table 2 displays a non-exhaustive list of regional and subregional intergovernmental IOs (some of which display specialized mandates) that are coordinating adaptation activities with UNFCCC mechanisms (UNFCCC, n.d.a). This is an area which is underexplored in the scholarship.

Table 2 Intergovernmental organizations at the regional level

Africa	Asia	Latin America
African Development Bank (AfDB)	Asian Development Bank (ADB)	Amazon Cooperation Treaty Organization (ACTO)
African Union (AU)	Asia Pacific Economic Cooperation (APEC)	Andean Community General Secretariat (CAN)
The Lake Chad Basin Commission (CBLT)	The Association of Southeast Asian Nations (ASEAN)	Central American Commission for Environment and Development (CCAD)
The Indian Ocean Commission (IOC)	Central Asia Regional Economic Cooperation (CAREC)	Caribbean Community Climate Change Centre (CCCCC)
	Coral Triangle Initiative on Coral Reefs, Fisheries and Food Security (CTI-CFF)	Inter-American Institute for Global Change Research (IAI)
	Economic Cooperation Organization (ECO)	Inter-American Development Bank (IADB)
	Mekong River Commission for Sustainable Development (MRC)	
	Pacific Islands Forum Secretariat (PIFS)	

5.4 Non-state and Sub-state Actors

The past decade has seen a 'Cambrian explosion' of transnational climate initiatives by non- and sub-state actors, ranging from private businesses to cities to multi-stakeholder partnerships (Abbott, 2012: 571). As Green (2014) notes, these actors often take on roles usually reserved for public authorities by creating, implementing and enforcing climate standards and regulations. It is increasingly acknowledged that such initiatives are vital to closing the global emissions gap and keeping global warming to 2 °C or less (Kuramochi et al., 2019). Beyond mitigation, scholars have begun to also examine the role of this class of actors – often closer to the ground – in accelerating a more global and transnational governance of adaptation (Persson and Dzebo, 2019).

5.4.1 Integrating Sub- and Non-state Actors into the Post-Paris Climate Change Regime

It is not just the growing size, scope and ambition of sub- and non-state action that is significant, but also their enhanced integration into the new post-Paris climate regime (Hale, 2016). In the wake of the 2009 Copenhagen summit, the pluralization of climate action was widely perceived as 'emerg[ing] from and contribut[ing] to the erosion of consensus around a megamultilateral response to climate change' (Hoffmann, 2011: 9). However, under the Paris Agreement, this trend seems to have been reversed. A series of UNFCCC-led orchestration efforts under the Global Climate Action Agenda (GCAA), first initiated in 2014 (see Table 3), have facilitated dialogue, knowledge exchange and cooperation among state, sub-state and non-state actors (Chan and Amling, 2019), resulting in a hybridization of the previously strictly multilateral climate regime (Bäckstrand et al., 2017). Indeed, Hale (2017: 1999) argues that 'one of the great innovations of the Paris model . . . was to embrace the diffusion of climate policy to multiple fora and to situate the UNFCCC as a central node in an increasingly complex governance ecosystem'.

A recent assessment by Chan et al. (2018) suggests that non-state climate initiatives have indeed started to deliver, albeit with significant differences between action areas and clear geographical biases in terms of participation, leadership and implementation. Much-needed adaptation action in developing countries remains underrepresented (Chan and Amling, 2019). In addition, observers have identified a range of factors that restrict the effectiveness of non-state action, including underfunding, vague commitments and the lack of comprehensive and consistent monitoring, reporting and verification (MRV) procedures to track compliance (Hsu et al., 2015; Michaelowa and Michaelowa, 2017; Chan et al., 2018). Others have pointed to democratic shortfalls of UNFCCC orchestration efforts (Bäckstrand and Kuyper, 2017), as well as the fact that the GCAA process remains relatively detached from multilateral negotiations (Hermwille, 2018). Finally, some have cautioned that a shift towards more non-state engagement 'may also release State actors from their public responsibility to act and could further unwarranted privatization of governance' (Chan, Brandi and Bauer, 2016: 239).

5.4.2 Cities and Other Sub-state Authorities

The role of subnational authorities in the global fight against climate change has received much attention in recent years. Because subnational administrations 'are often closer to climate problems – and to the solutions – than the UNFCCC

Table 3 Integrating non-state and sub-state climate action into the UNFCCC process

September 2014	**UN Climate Summit** Hosted by UN Secretary-General Ban Ki-moon, the 2014 Climate Summit brought together leaders from government, finance, business and civil society, as well as subnational authorities to catalyze ambitious action and encourage new climate commitments, prior to COP-20 and COP-21 (UN News, 2014).
December 2014	**COP-20 in Lima** The opening of the UNFCCC regime to non-state action was officially set in motion with the launch of the Lima–Paris Action Agenda (LPAA) at COP-20. A joint undertaking of the Peruvian and French COP presidencies, the Office of the UN Secretary-General and the UNFCCC Secretariat, the LPAA aimed to 'galvanize the groundswell of climate actions' from cities, regions, private businesses and civil society organizations (Chan et al., 2015: 469). To showcase these actions, the Peruvian COP presidency launched the Non-state Actor Zone for Climate Action (NAZCA), which quickly became 'the broadest international compilation of non-state commitments to climate action' (Wei, 2016: 2). It currently records over 14,500 actors representing over 22,400 initiatives (NAZCA, n.d.).
November – December 2015	**COP-21 in Paris** At COP-21 in Paris, several high-profile initiatives by non-party stakeholders were showcased and announced in the context of the LPAA, framed by the French presidency as the 'fourth pillar of the Paris Agreement' (Hermwille, 2018: 457). The COP formally acknowledged commitments made by non-state and sub-state actors through decision 1/CP.21, reaffirming the importance of the LPAA and NAZCA (UNFCCC, 2016). It also decided to continue and expand the LPAA process, through a series of annual events led by two 'high-level champions' through to 2020.

Table 3 (cont.)

November 2016	**COP-22 in Marrakech** At COP-22, the Global Climate Action Agenda (GCAA) – also known as the Marrakech Partnership for Global Climate Action – was launched to continue the LPAA process and support 'implementation of the Paris Agreement by enabling collaboration between governments and the cities, regions, businesses and investors that must act on climate change' (UNFCCC, n.d.c). Action under the GCAAA is organized across seven thematic areas: land use, oceans and coastal zones, water, human settlements, transport, energy and industry.
November 2017	**COP-23 in Bonn under the Presidency of Fiji** Under the GCAA, six days of parallel thematic sessions and high-level events were organized at COP-23 to scale up transnational climate initiatives and strengthen collaboration between UNFCCC parties and non-parties (UNFCCC, n.d.d). The COP also saw the launch of the first *Yearbook of Climate Action*, which highlights the achievements made under the GCAA. Significantly, non-state actors were also invited to contribute directly to the Talanoa Dialogue, launched at COP-23, to assess and enhance collective efforts towards achieving the long-term goal of the Paris Agreement. Indeed, some have concluded that 'the Talanoa Dialogue can be seen as the most concrete effort to involve non-state actors in the formal decision-making process of the UNFCCC to date' (Nyman and Stainforth, 2018).
September 2018	**Global Climate Action Summit** Convened by Governor Jerry Brown and the State of California, the Global Climate Action Summit showcased the increasing scale and scope of climate action and commitments from regions, cities, businesses, investors and civil society, with the aim of inspiring more ambitious action from state and non-state actors. The Summit mobilized over 500 new commitments to climate action. This demonstration of continued leadership from non-state actors, was particularly significant in light of US withdrawal from the Paris Agreement (Arroyo, 2018).

December 2018

COP-24 in Katowice

COP-24 saw eight days of dialogues and events under the umbrella of the GCAA, as well as the announcement of major pledges by non-state and sub-state actors. However, these activities continued to run separately from the intergovernmental negotiations (Obergassel et al., 2019). The Paris rulebook, adopted by COP-24, did not specify a clear role for non-state actors, leading observers to conclude that '[w]hile there is an ever-growing expectation that the private sector will come up with the sort of ambition governments are lacking, there is surprisingly little regulatory space in the Paris Agreement for non-state actors to gain hold' (Streck, von Unger and Krämer, 2019: 187).

Climate Action Summit

Hosted by UN Secretary-General António Guterres, the 2019 UN Climate Action Summit, brought together leaders from government, civil society and the private sector to raise ambition and create stronger links between state and non-state climate action. For the first time, the UN also convened a Youth Climate Summit, aimed at strengthening the voice of young people on the need to tackle climate change. Although the Climate Action Summit saw the launch of some striking non-state initiatives, observers noted that 'most of the major economies fell woefully short' with regard to enhancing their climate pledges (Andrew Steer qtd. in Farand, 2019). Concerns have also been raised about the future of the GCAA process, which will end in 2020. A number of non-party stakeholders have therefore called upon COP-25 to renew and update the institutional arrangements that have developed under the GCAA (Hale, 2019).

September 2019

parties themselves', they are key actors in national implementation processes (Duggan, 2019: 2). Increasingly, however, subnational authorities such as cities, states, regions or provinces, are taking on roles beyond implementation, generating their own policies and regulations for climate change mitigation and adaptation (Finck, 2014). They often do so despite, or in response to, a lack of ambitious climate action on the national level. For example, after US President Trump announced his intention to withdraw from the Paris Agreement, governors across the country came together to form the United States Climate Alliance, which is committed to enhancing mitigation action in accordance with the Paris Agreement goals (Umbers and Moss, 2019).

In many EU countries, subnational authorities have adopted more ambitious mitigation targets than their national governments (The Climate Group, 2018). Cities, in particular, have emerged as key players in bottom-up climate 'experimentation' (Acuto, 2013; Smeds and Acuto, 2018). Not only are many cities – and especially their most vulnerable populations – at high risk from climate change; they are also major contributors to the problem, accounting for over 75 per cent of global CO_2 emissions (Appleby, 2019). With run-away urbanization, the centrality of cities in responding to climate change will only increase in the future.[6] In July 2019, 300 European cities declared a climate emergency at a municipal level opening the way for the adoption of more powers to curb the effects of climate change. In the same month, New York became the largest city on earth to adopt mandatory carbon reduction targets for all major buildings (Barnard, 2019).

Subnational climate actions are often supported through networks, such as the C40 Climate Leadership Group, Local Governments for Sustainability (ICLEI), United Cities and Local Governments (UCLG), R20 – Regions of Climate Action, or the Compact of Mayors. These networks support learning and exchange as well as the development of norms, practices and standards. They also facilitate linkages with the UNFCCC regime and partnerships with other transnational actors, such as private businesses and civil society (Lin, 2018). Over the past years, these networks have grown substantially in number and scope. Acuto and Rayner (2016) offer one of the most recent and most comprehensive mappings of the global landscape of city networks, covering 170 such networks across the world.

A key message that urban leaders have sought to convey is that 'nations talk, cities act' (Curtis, 2014: 4). Cities and other subnational actors are now widely viewed as holding much promise for advancing global climate governance in

---

[6] By 2050, 68 per cent of the world's population is projected to reside in urban areas (UN DESA, 2019).

the absence of sufficiently ambitious national action. However, as van der Heijden et al. (2018: 365) point out, 'there remains a worrying lack of robust evidence for their effectiveness and ability to fulfil this role.' First, tracking and evaluating subnational commitments can be difficult because of their voluntary and (often) vague nature, as well as their diversity, highlighting the need to make initiatives more concrete and comparable (IVM, 2015). Concerns have also been raised about the unequal power relationships within transnational networks of subnational authorities, with actors from the Global South struggling to make their voices heard – even in nominally inclusive networks (Bouteligier, 2012). Finally, observers have highlighted the risk of overestimating the agency, authority and independence of subnational actors, while underestimating how their own politics are shaped by carbon lock-in (van der Heijden et al., 2018). As Umbers and Moss (2019: 2) point out, we should not assume that cities, states, regions or provinces are automatically more progressive: 'some sub-national political communities have not merely failed to act, but have also sought to frustrate efforts to address climate change'.

5.4.3 Non-governmental Organizations

Non-governmental organizations (NGOs), activist groups and other grassroots actors have played an important role in raising understanding and public awareness of climate change since the very beginning. As the climate change threat grew more and more urgent, a broad transnational climate movement emerged, calling for decisive and socially just climate action on the local, regional, national and global level (Garrelts and Dietz, 2013). Members of this movement have become increasingly visible during the annual climate summits, both inside the conference halls (as observers) and outside (as protesters). This is reflected, for example, in the number of UNFCCC-accredited NGOs, which rose more than tenfold between 1995 and 2015 (see Figure 3). Whereas early engagement was led primarily by Northern environmental NGOs with extensive technical expertise, the group of civil society actors involved in global climate politics has become much more diverse over time, in particular in light of the increasing engagement of justice- and development-focused groups (Busby and Hadden, 2014). To coordinate their participation within the UNFCCC regime, NGOs often participate in informal transnational networks, such as the Climate Action Network (CAN).

Because of their limited economic and coercive power, transnational NGOs have traditionally relied on advocacy activities to initiative change (Keck and Sikkink, 1998). This includes both 'cooperative' strategies, focused on agenda setting, knowledge generation/dissemination and persuasion, as well as more

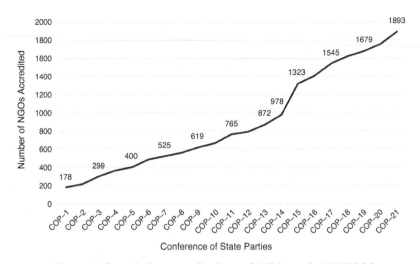

Figure 3 Cumulative accreditations of NGOs at the UNFCCC

Source: based on Gereke and Brühl (2019: 879)

'adversarial' strategies, such as 'naming and shaming' or litigation (Brown, Ebrahim and Batliwala, 2012). The latter has become an increasingly popular strategy in the climate change domain, with more than 1,300 cases identified in at least 28 jurisdictions, many filed or supported by NGOs (Setzer and Byrnes, 2019). NGOs have also taken on more varied roles beyond advocacy, for example, as service providers and 'governance entrepreneurs' in the area of carbon disclosure or as implementing partners in multi-stakeholder climate projects (Pattberg, 2017; Gray and Purdy, 2018). An example is CDP (formerly known as the Carbon Disclosure Project) which works with some of the world's largest companies on disclosing their environmental impacts (CDP, n.d.). CDP is also a founding partner of the Science Based Targets initiative (SBTi), a partnership which encourages companies to set emission reduction targets that are in line with science and the Paris Agreement's long-term mitigation goal. Beyond such activities by legacy NGOs, more radical and less formal activist movements have also sprung up in the climate change domain, spearheaded by Extinction Rebellion and the Fridays for Future strikes inspired by Greta Thunberg.

NGOs and other civil society actors have played a key role in raising public awareness on climate change and pushing the issue up the global political agenda. They have also been instrumental in reshaping the normative framing of the climate change discussion, for example, by highlighting its human rights dimensions (Dyck, 2017). However, their authority remains limited, primarily because of their lack of resources and coercive power. Multi-stakeholder part-nerships can provide a source of additional resources and political influence but may also pose a danger to NGOs' autonomy and critical capacity (Baur and Schmitz, 2012). Within the UNFCCC process, NGOs have gradually gained more opportunities to engage with climate change negotiations, yet they remain excluded from key stages of the process. This was particularly obvious at COP-21 in Paris, where civil society observers were subjected to unprecedented restrictions and unable to follow key parts of the negotiations (Doelle, 2016; Orr, 2016). There also remains a significant geographical bias in terms of NGO representation at the UNFCCC: around three-quarters of NGOs accredited to observe international climate negotiations come from the Global North (Gereke and Brühl, 2019). Finally, NGOs today face an action context that is radically different from previous decades: while more players than ever acknowledge the need to address climate change, collective action falls woefully short. Thus, Berny and Rootes (2018) argue that environmental NGOs may be 'at a crossroads' where they need to rethink their strategies, going beyond the binary choice of radicalism versus reform.

5.4.4 Private Business Actors

As major sources of GHG emissions, private businesses have an important role to play in shaping a low carbon-future. Whereas the early days of the global climate change regime were marked by anti-regulatory lobbying efforts by private businesses, led by the fossil fuel industry, the past two decades have seen a rapid diversification of business interests (Falkner, 2010). While private-led institutions and have developed mostly bottom-up, they frequently use the international climate regime as a point of reference. Green (2014), for instance, maps nearly thirty private carbon accounting standards that in one way or another align themselves with the standards set out under the UNFCCC's CDM. The result is a hybrid network of private rules using public rules as 'anchors'.

Rather than a regulatory burden, corporate climate action is increasingly seen as an opportunity to reap reputational benefits and increase resource efficiency (Vandenbergh and Gilligan, 2017). Even major fossil fuel companies are now recognizing 'the significance of climate change' (Shell, n.d.). A number of leading companies have committed to serious climate action, often in the absence of direct regulatory pressure, for example, by adopting specific emis-sion reduction targets, increasing energy efficiency, switching to renewable energy sources or committing to zero deforestation. Laggards may face pressure from activists and consumers but also from investors, in light of growing evidence 'that companies that are able to manage environmental risks and opportunities better than their peers tend to out-perform them financially as well' (Labatt and White, 2007: 111). Supply chain governance can also play a major role in pressuring companies into increasing their environmental performance (Haufler, 2018).

A variety of new global networks and platforms have emerged to catalyze and coordinate business and investor action, such as the We Mean Business coalition or Climate Action 100+. There is also a growing number of sector-specific initiatives and networks. In areas where no legal regulation exists, private standards, certification schemes and other transparency initiatives often serve as the key mechanism of defining, measuring and rewarding businesses' climate performance. For example, the most widely used standard for GHG emissions accounting at the company level (the Greenhouse Gas Protocol Corporate Accounting and Reporting Standard) has been developed not by public authorities but by two NGOs, in consultation with other stakeholders (Green, 2010). Private actors also play a key role in the reporting and disclosure of corporate climate action (Gupta and Mason, 2016; Pattberg, 2017). While this does not necessarily reflect a decline of public authority, it is testament of 'the changing role of states as a collective governing body and the increasing complexity of governance arrangements' (Green, 2014: 163).

Private actors are increasingly expected to contribute to resolving global public goods problems. However, addressing 'wicked' problems like climate change through private action requires revisiting prominent efficiency assumptions regarding market mechanisms, without losing sight of normative concerns of power hierarchy, accountability and representation. While private climate action may be best placed to harness the efficiency advantages of market mechanisms, concerns persist regarding accountability and representation (Andonova and Levy, 2003). 'Greenwashing' is maybe the most obvious concern with regard to business-driven climate action. Privately governed initiatives 'may aim to reap the reputational benefits of producing public goods without actually doing so', producing weak standards that promote a race to the bottom instead of a race to the top (Green, 2014: 177).

Researchers have identified a number of factors driving voluntary corporate commitments, ranging from efforts to pre-empt regulation, secure first-mover advantages, respond to investor pressure and reap reputational benefits to non-profit-driven motivations. Less is known about the actual impact of such voluntary commitments (Marx and Wouters, 2015). Voluntary certification schemes and transparency initiatives may lead to substitution effects, where firms prioritize easily measured superficial dimensions over costly and more fundamental performance dimensions (Berliner and Prakash, 2015). Much of the available data is disclosed on a voluntary basis and collected, processed and distributed by other non-state actors, primarily NGOs. This raises important questions about the legitimacy and viability of transparency-based governance and its ultimate effectiveness in promoting greater accountability and sustainability (Lebaron and Lister, 2015).

Overall, the business sector possesses superior financial resources and strong organizational capacity, particularly when compared to environmental NGOs, and is well placed to exploit the privileged access it has to key governmental actors. Many professionals within the private sector fully accept the gravity of the situation, acknowledging that 'in a contest between physics and politics, physics will always win'.[7] However, the business community remains split when it comes to responding to the climate crisis. Indeed, some of the largest asset management companies, such as BlackRock and Vanguard, which together control more than USD 11.2 trillion worth of assets, continue to use their shareholder voting power to undermine investor action on climate change (Helmore, 2019). This has led some scholars to question whether Western countries, in particular, 'have the right kind of private sector' to address global catastrophic risks such as climate change (McLeod, 2010). Florini identifies the single-minded focus on short-term profit maximization as a structural obstacle to effective private sector provision of global public goods, with Anglo-Saxon business schools perpetuating the idea that the fiduciary responsibility of any corporation is, first and foremost, to maximize shareholder value (GGI, 2018).

5.4.5 Public–Private Initiatives

Over the past twenty years, and in particular since the World Summit for Sustainable Development (WSSD) in 2002, public–private partnerships (PPPs) have proliferated in diverse areas of global governance, such as health, human rights, the environment and sustainable development, creating a new type of 'hybrid' governance to complement multilateral and purely private initiatives (Andonova, 2017). Transnational PPPs can be defined as 'voluntary agreements between public actors (IOs, states, or sub-state public authorities) and non-state actors ([NGOs], companies, foundations, etc.) on a set of governance objectives and norms, rules, practices, or implementation procedures and their attainment across multiple jurisdictions and levels of governance' (Andonova, 2017: 2).

In the face of increasingly complex problems – climate change being a prime example – PPPs are often seen as 'the best chance of bringing the necessary resources, technology, and commitment to ensuring a sustainable future for the

---

[7] Quote from NGO analyst, recalling conversation with high-level corporate executives.

planet' (Gray and Purdy, 2018: 152). The UN system has endorsed PPPs as an integral part of twenty-first century global governance, most recently through the Sustainable Development Goals (SDGs), which designate PPPs as a key 'means of implementation' (SDG Knowledge Platform, n.d.). PPPs are thus 'firmly embedded within the normative structures of the UN' (Pattberg, 2010: 281). Prominent examples of PPPs in the climate change domain include the Renewable Energy and Energy Efficiency Partnership (REEEP), the Global Methane Initiative (GMI) or REN21 (Renewable Energy Policy Network for the 21st Century). Initiating actors are often national governments or international organizations, although Bulkeley et al. (2014: 74) also find 'considerable entrepreneurship on the part of non-state actors in initiating partnership arrangements.' PPPs are recognized and promoted under the UNFCCC's Global Climate Action Agenda (GCAA), with NAZCA currently listing over 120 'cooperative initiatives' (NAZCA, n.d.).

Transnational PPPs are often viewed as promising and innovative tools to deliver global public goods, given their potential to create 'win-win solutions that increase problem-solving capacity and serve as a response to both state and market failure' (Bexell and Mörth, 2010: 15). However, research has not found consistent evidence of positive performance of PPPs.[8] Concerns have also been voiced over the lack of clearly defined goals as well as reliable accountability, transparency and compliance mechanisms (Bäckstrand, 2008; Mert, 2015). Power imbalances within PPPs are another concern, potentially leading to the exclusion or co-optation of civil society and Global South partners. A recent analysis of NAZCA-registered partnerships found that they display significant geographical imbalances, with only 22 per cent of participants coming from non-OECD countries (Chan et al., 2018). Finally, as with other non-IGO activities, there is a danger of diverting attention and resources away from more inclusive multilateral arrangements. For example, as Andonova (2017: 4) observes, '[t]he World Bank partnerships for climate finance have drawn scrutiny for creating a parallel structure with asymmetric influence of donor countries, compared to the more broadly representative process under [UNFCCC]'.

6 Global Architecture of the Climate Change Regime

Years of multilateral gridlock – and the sheer complexity of the climate change challenge, which spills over into many other issue domains – have contributed

---

[8] Analyzing more than 340 partnerships for sustainable development, registered in conjunction with the 2002 WSSD, Pattberg and Widerberg (2016) find that only a quarter of these partnerships produce comprehensive outputs that match their publicly stated goals and ambitions.

to the institutional hybridization and fragmentation of the climate change regime. As Section 5 has demonstrated, the cast of actors within this regime complex has grown and diversified significantly over the past two decades. This section locates this actor mapping within the global climate change 'regime complex' and identifies the promise of the Paris Agreement for galvanizing new pathways to global-to-local climate policy implementation.

6.1 The Global Climate Change Regime Complex

There is no *one* global regime for climate change but rather a 'regime complex', a set of more or less closely coupled regulatory regimes that may overlap, complement or conflict with each other (Keohane and Victor, 2011). Scholars have provided detailed mappings of how the structure of global climate governance has changed from a mono-centric regime – with the UNFCCC at the top – towards a polycentric regime complex with multiple centres of authority (Widerberg, 2016; Widerberg, Pattberg and Kristensen, 2016). What we observe in the climate change regime complex (Figure 4) is an array of regulatory elements that is only partially organized hierarchically.

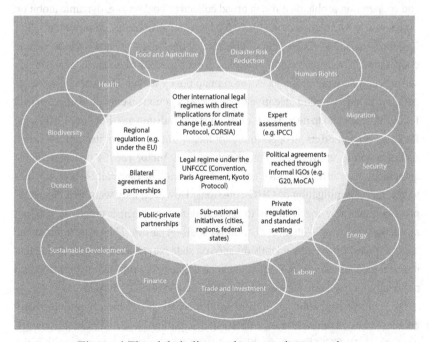

Figure 4 The global climate change regime complex

Source: Inspired by Keohane and Victor (2011: 9). CORSIA = Carbon Offsetting and Reduction Scheme for International Aviation; MoCA = Ministerial on Climate Action

The fragmentation of global climate governance is partly a direct consequence of the complexity of the 'problem [which] is interlinked in both cause and effect with most areas of human activity' (van Asselt 2007: ii). In other words, the multidimensional nature of climate change makes it impossible to address it through a single, well-demarcated and fully integrated regime. This poses difficult challenges for the creation of institutional arrangements capable of exploiting synergies and managing potential conflict between different problem dimensions (e.g. mitigation and adaptation) or governance domains (e.g. climate change and energy security). Yet, climate change does not only pose difficult *coordination* problems but also a series of *cooperation* problems. To a large degree, the fragmentation of global climate governance is a reflection of significant power shifts in the global economic system that have redrawn and deepened interstate divisions (Timmons 2011). In this context, the proliferation of different rules and institutions is often in the interest of powerful actors, allowing them to increase or perpetuate their dominance at the international level by choosing the platforms that suit them best (Drezner, 2009) or making it difficult for weaker states to come to agreement on any particular issue (Benvenisti and Downs 2007).

The Paris Agreement presents a pragmatic attempt to address both coordination and cooperation problems through broad collective goal setting, dynamic ambition cycles and a shift towards national pledges and procedural commitments. For Keohane and Victor (2016), the significance of the Paris Agreement for deepening cooperation within the regime complex is its potential to enhance transparency surrounding national preferences for climate policy action. However, most states continue to have a strong incentive to avoid costly action on climate change, to wait for others to act and to negotiate for self-interested advantages. For Hale (2017), the Paris Agreement offers an opportunity for the regime to reinvent itself in a way that makes a virtue of fragmentation. Keohane and Victor (2016) concur that the agreement does offer scope for enhanced cooperation, especially when it comes to accelerating mitigation of GHG emissions. However, they warn that the agreement contains few mechanisms to prevent defection when it comes to tackling problems which imply unequal distributive costs on parties. They also highlight the dangers posed by the agreement's reliance on state party self-reporting, noting that national pledges 'vary in the extent to which they contain misleading promises and politically motivated information' (Keohane and Victor, 2016: 572).

By institutionalizing a 'hybrid multilateralism', which simultaneously enables and constrains non-state actor participation in global climate governance, the UNFCCC has re-established itself as a centre of gravity within the regime complex, albeit one that is 'catalytic' rather than regulatory (Bäckstrand et al., 2017; Kuyper, Linnér and Schroeder, 2018; Hale, 2017). However, to be effective, this bottom-up logic requires both preference alignment among powerful actors, as well as sufficient institutional capacity on the national level. The Paris Agreement's success ultimately hinges on whether domestic structures are in place to support is implementation by increasing ambition, encouraging innovation and ensuring transparency and accountability of state and non-state climate action. It is to the crucial domain of global-to-local climate policy implementation that the analysis now turns.

6.2 Global Climate Governance through State Reform: Local Pathways to Policy Implementation

The innovative crux of the 2015 Paris Agreement is that it embraces the polycentric architecture of the global climate change regime complex. Rather than attempting to resurrect Kyoto-style 'megamultilateralism' (Hoffmann, 2011) as the basic governance model for tackling climate change, it acknowledges that bottom-up national action, combined with subnational and private experimentation, may be the most realistic approach to keeping global warming to 1.5–2 °C. This new bottom-up governance logic is supported by complexity theory, which suggests that fragmentation and hybridization – if it allows for bottom-up innovation, learning and fail-safe experimentation – may be the best way forward when it comes to addressing problems as wicked as climate change (Homer-Dixon, 2007; Snowden and Boone, 2007; Harrison and Geyer, 2019).

However, the Paris Agreement's success ultimately hinges on national preferences for action and sufficient local institutional capacity to ensure effective policy implementation. Good climate laws are an essential ingredient to 'lock in' climate commitments and send credible signals to investors and other shareholders about long-term decarbonization efforts (Manguiat and Raine, 2018). These must be accompanied by robust national frameworks to ensure monitoring, reporting and verification (MRV) of emissions levels, climate policies and finance. Equally importantly, there must be ways to hold governments – and private actors – to account over their climate change policies and push for more ambitious action. As the Paris Agreement itself does not establish a strong compliance regime, national institutions and civil society engagement will be key to ensuring that states stick to their pledges (Karlsson-Vinkhuyzen et al., 2017). As discussed further in the following, a promising development may be the emergence of independent national advisory bodies across the world, many of which do not just provide concrete science-based advice but also evaluate progress made on climate action.

At the present time, installation of effective domestic structures for climate policy implementation is highly uneven, especially in many developing countries, which have made emission reduction commitments for the first time and accepted new procedural requirements. Policy designers in the Global South also lack guidance from metagovernance structures such as the EU, which plays a key role in coordinating implementation of the Paris Agreement in its member states. Thus, in addition to refining the Agreement's rulebook and enhancing ambition, upcoming negotiations must 'grapple with how to ensure developing countries have adequate financial, human and technological resources to deliver on their climate commitments and follow the Rulebook's reporting guidelines' (Cogswell and Dagnet, 2019). In the long-term, a key provision of the Paris Agreement might help fuel domestic capacity-building, both in developed and developing countries, namely the requirement to regularly update and strengthen NDCs. Höhne et al. (2017) find that the preparation of the first round of NDCs 'contributed to the development of processes and institutions for national climate policy-making'. Thus, subsequent ambition cycles may further encourage procedural and institutional innovation on the domestic level.

The remaining parts of this section focus on two examples of domestic institutional structures that can play a key role in implementing the Paris Agreement and enhancing national climate action: (1) MRV systems, specifically the preparation of national inventories of GHG emissions and removals, and (2) independent national advisory bodies on climate change.

6.2.1 Monitoring, Reporting and Verification (MRV) under the Paris Agreement

MRV has emerged as a key concept in global climate change governance and an important issue in international climate negotiations. Its main function is to enhance transparency, accountability and, ultimately, effectiveness of climate action by tracking GHG emissions levels, mitigation or adaptation policies and projects and/or the support received for such actions. While negotiations under the UNFCCC are primarily concerned with national MRV frameworks (Figure 5), MRV activities may be carried out beyond and below the national level, e.g. by cities or private businesses (Singh, Finnegan and Levin, 2016).

The term MRV first appeared in the 2007 Bali Action Plan (UNFCCC, 2008), yet basic elements of an international MRV framework have been in place since the very beginning of the UNFCCC regime, with the Convention requesting parties to regularly prepare and report 'national inventories' of GHG emissions and removals (United Nations, 1992). Over time, these arrangements have evolved into a comprehensive MRV framework. However, up until now, reporting requirements for developed (Annex I) countries have differed significantly from those of developing countries in accordance with the CBDR–RC principle (UNFCCC, n.d.b).

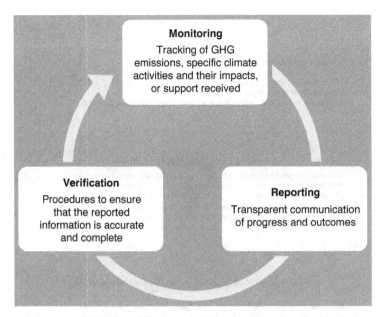

Figure 5 MRV under the Paris Agreement
Source: based on information obtained from UNFCCC

This is now changing. The 2015 Paris Agreement establishes universal and harmonized MRV provisions under the Enhanced Transparency Framework (ETF) (see Figure 6). The ETF is applicable to all parties, although it still provides flexibility 'to those developing country parties that need it in the light of their capacities' (UNFCCC, 2015). A fundamental feature is the regular provision by each party of biennial transparency reports (BTRs), which must include a national inventory of GHG emissions and removals, as well as other information necessary to track progress made on NDCs and support provided or received. Reported information will be subject to a technical expert review as well as a facilitative, multilateral consideration of progress. A set of modalities, procedures and guidelines (MPGs), agreed upon in 2018, sketch how the ETF will be put into practical operation (UNFCCC, 2019c). Parties need to submit their first BTRs by 31 December 2024.

6.2.2 The Role of Independent National Advisory Bodies

A relatively recent phenomenon is the emergence of national-level independent bodies, tasked with offering science-based advice, providing input to national climate strategies, contributing to public dialogue and holding governments to account for implementing climate change policies (Averchenkova, 2019). In

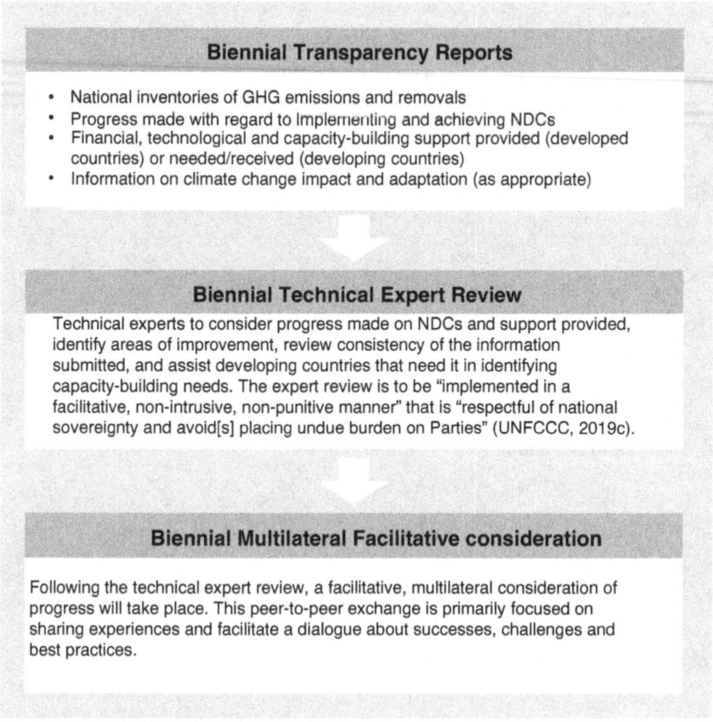

Biennial Transparency Reports

- National inventories of GHG emissions and removals
- Progress made with regard to Implementing and achieving NDCs
- Financial, technological and capacity-building support provided (developed countries) or needed/received (developing countries)
- Information on climate change impact and adaptation (as appropriate)

Biennial Technical Expert Review

Technical experts to consider progress made on NDCs and support provided, identify areas of improvement, review consistency of the information submitted, and assist developing countries that need it in identifying capacity-building needs. The expert review is to be "implemented in a facilitative, non-intrusive, non-punitive manner" that is "respectful of national sovereignty and avoid[s] placing undue burden on Parties" (UNFCCC, 2019c).

Biennial Multilateral Facilitative consideration

Following the technical expert review, a facilitative, multilateral consideration of progress will take place. This peer-to-peer exchange is primarily focused on sharing experiences and facilitate a dialogue about successes, challenges and best practices.

Figure 6 The Paris Agreement's Enhanced Transparency Framework
Source: based on information obtained from UNFCCC

particular, the diffusion of long-term climate framework laws (Duwe et al., 2017) has propelled the establishment of a growing number of national advisory councils, committees or panels, mostly in the EU (see Table 4) but also in other regions of the world, including in low- and middle-income countries. To our knowledge, no formal global network or authoritative overview of independent national advisory bodies exists to date. Our review is therefore based on an extensive multi-language Google keyword search, supplemented by information available from the Climate Change Laws of the World Database (www.climate-laws.org), administered by the LSE's Grantham Research Institute on Climate Change and the Environment, and a recent explorative study conducted by the Finnish Climate Change Panel (Weaver, Lötjönen and Ollikainen, 2019). New bodies are still emerging, so the compilation provided in Table 4 is not necessarily comprehensive. A commonly used definition of national advisory bodies does not yet exist and there are no official principles to guide their legal and institutional set-up. However, there are signs of policy diffusion and learning, in particular within the EU. As such, there is ample scope for future research to map and

Table 4 Independent Advisory Councils in the European Union (UK included)

Country	Established	Name of Body	Website
Austria	Set up in 2012 through the Climate Change Act 2011 (which was amended in 2017)	National Climate Protection Advisory Board (*Nationaler Klimaschutzbeirat*, NKB)	www.bmnt.gv.at/english/envir onment/Climateprotect/The-Austrian-Climate-Change-Act.html Note: There is no official website or any other evidence of NKB activity.
Belgium	Set up in 1997 and amended in 2010	The Federal Council for Sustainable Development (*Federale Raad voor Duurzame Ontwikkeling or Conseil Fédéral du Développement Durable – FRDO-CFDD*)	www.frdo-cfdd.be
Denmark	2015 through the 2014 Danish Climate Act	Climate Council (*Klimarådet*)	www.klimaraadet.dk
Finland	Officially 2016 through the 2015 Finnish Climate Change Act (a body of the same name had been operational since 2012)	Climate Change Panel (*Suomen ilmastopaneeli*)	www.ilmastopaneeli.fi

Table 4 (cont.)

Country	Established	Name of Body	Website
France	Created 2019 by Presidential decree	High Council for Climate (*Haut Conseil pour le Climat*)	www.hautconseilclimat.fr
	2013 by decree	Council for Ecological Transition (*Conseil national de la transition écologique – CNTE*) Note: This body serves primarily as a forum for debate between various stakeholders on issues related to the environment and sustainable development.	www.ecologique-solidaire.gouv.fr/cnte
Germany	1972 through a 1971 Decree	Advisory Council on the Environment (*Sachverständigenrat für Umweltfragen – SRU*)	www.umweltrat.de/EN/home/home_node.html
	1992	Advisory Council on Global Change (*Wissenschaftlicher Beirat der Bundesregierung Globale Umweltveränderungen, WBGU*)	www.wbgu.de/en

Hungary	1995 through the Environmental Act	National Environmental Council of Hungary (*Országos Környezetvédelmi Tanács*)	www.oktt.hu
Ireland	2016 under the Climate Action and Low Carbon Development Act 2015	Climate Change Advisory Council	www.climatecouncil.ie
Portugal	1997 by Decree-Law No. 221/97	National Council on Sustainable Development and Environment (*Conselho Nacional do Ambiente e do Desenvolvimento Sustentável – CNADS*)	www.cnads.pt
Spain	1994 by Royal Decree (with various reforms since)	Environment Advisory Council (*Consejo Asesor del Medio Ambiente – CAMA*)	www.miteco.gob.es/es/ministerio/funciones-estructura/otros-organismos-organizaciones/cama
Sweden	2018 under the 2017 Climate Policy Framework	Climate Policy Council (*Klimatpolitiska Rådet*)	www.klimatpolitiskaradet.se
United Kingdom	2008 through the Climate Change Act 2008	UK Committee on Climate Change	www.theccc.org.uk

Source: based on Weaver, Lötjönen and Ollikainen (2019) and supplementary data from the Climate Change Laws of the World Database

explain the global diffusion of independent climate advisory bodies, with a focus on common features and, crucially, key determinants of success.

Within the EU, most of the bodies we identified have been set up over the past decade through national climate change and energy transition laws. There are also a few advisory councils, set up in the 1990s or even earlier, that address broader issues related to the environment or sustainable development and have taken on climate change as part of their advisory duties. Almost all of these bodies enjoy at least partial independence from governments and have a formal mandate aimed at enabling policymakers to take informed, science-based decisions and implement them. They can potentially play a key role in driving ambitious and consistent national climate action as well as enhancing transparency, accountability and social acceptability of specific policies and targets. However, they have not inspired much comparative analysis to date, perhaps because they do not constitute a clearly defined category and the trend of setting up such bodies is not yet consolidated. Our own exploratory review of independent advisory bodies in the EU suggests that they share many similarities but also display variations along a number of parameters:

- *Thematic remit*: All advisory bodies that were established in the EU since 2008, mostly in Northern Europe, have a purely climate-oriented mandate. Most address both mitigation and adaptation related concerns, and the UK Committee of Climate Change has even established a dedicated adaptation subcommittee. Older advisory bodies, mostly in Western, Central and Southern Europe, have a wider remit. For example, the German Advisory Council on the Environment, which has existed since 1972, covers a broad array of 'environmental conditions, problems, and political trends' (SRU, n.d.).

- *Membership selection*: Members are usually appointed by the government or relevant ministries for a fixed term, ranging from two years (in Finland) to six years (in Sweden), often with the possibility of being reappointed for a consecutive term. They may be nominated by public authorities, scientific institutions or previous post holders. In some cases, advisory bodies have 'ex-officio' members that are automatically entitled to a position on the council or committee, as is the case in Ireland (CCAC, n.d.).

- *Composition and stakeholder engagement:* The majority of bodies consists primarily of academic experts from a range of disciplines across the natural and social sciences. These experts may be joined by representatives from NGOs, the private sector or specific interest groups. Some advisory bodies also include government officials and members of public bodies. The number of members varies widely, from seven (Germany and Denmark) to over thirty (Portugal).

Some Councils regularly engage non-member stakeholders. In the case of the Danish Council on Climate Change, engagement of relevant parties (e.g. trade unions, companies, NGOs, municipalities and regions) is even mandated by legislation.

- *Mandate and powers:* The mandate and powers of advisory bodies in the EU are limited. While they often provide concrete policy advice and monitor progress, they cannot make policies or force governments to change their approach to climate change. In some countries (e.g. the UK and Denmark), the government has a statutory duty to respond to the annual progress reports prepared by the advisory councils. Beyond this, however, these bodies lack legislative teeth and, in order to drive change, they rely 'on the political embarrassment that [their] assessments may cause and the threat of a judicial review' (Averchenkova, Fankhauser and Finnegan, 2018: 4).
- *Number of support staff and budget:* Information on staff and budgets (where it is available) suggests that there is considerable variation across the EU. While some advisory bodies have very small secretariats that offer primarily administrative support, others have much larger secretariats that make substantial contributions to research, reporting and communication. With an average annual budget of around GBP 3.7 million and a secretariat of around thirty staff, the UK's Committee on Climate Change (CCC) appears to be the best-resourced independent advisory body (Averchenkova, Fankhauser and Finnegan, 2018).
- *Independence:* Because the influence of advisory bodies depends largely on their reputation, it is key for institutional structures to ensure objectivity and independence. Independence may be influenced by a range factors, including composition, reliability of funding, administrative set-up, appointment and removal procedures or length of mandate. For example, the inclusion of ex-officio members in the Irish Climate Change Advisory Council has raised concerns about independence (Torny, 2017). Legal basis may also be of relevance; for example, advisory bodies established by a legislative act may be better protected from threats of dissolution than those established by decree.

In theory, independent national advisory bodies can provide a 'safeguard against political mood swings', by taking a long-term, science-based view on national climate policies (Fankhauser, Averchenkova and Finnegan, 2018: 12). However, as experience from beyond Europe demonstrates, even a relatively strong institutional set-up does not guarantee a body's survival. The Australian Climate Commission, for example, which had been set up in 2011 (building on the UK model) was abolished two years later by the newly elected Abbott government, as part of its 'plans to streamline government processes and avoid duplication of services' (Hunt, 2013). A similar fate was suffered by the US

Advisory Committee for the Sustained National Climate Assessment, which was dismantled by the Trump administration in 2017. Remarkably, however, in both cases the body was resurrected. In the United States, the governor of New York, Andrew Cuomo helped reconvene the Committee (Waldman, 2019); in Australia, a public crowdfunding campaign ensured that the Climate Commission (now renamed the Climate Council) could continue its work (Yeo, 2013).

Case Study: The UK Climate Change Committee

The UK Committee on Climate Change (CCC) was established by the 2008 Climate Change Act. As 'a significant institutional innovation for implementation' (Benson and Lorenzoni, 2014: 2016), the CCC provides a mechanism to ensure that the long-term objectives set in the Act are being met. The CCC's institutional set-up is widely viewed as a good-practice example and it has provided inspiration for a many of the recently established bodies in the EU and beyond (Averchenkova, Fankhauser and Finnegan, 2018). The roles and responsibilities of the CCC, as set out in the Climate Change Act, include:

- Providing independent advice on climate change mitigation – in particular on appropriate national carbon budgets and targets – and climate change adaptation
- Monitoring progress on reducing emissions and enhancing climate resilience
- Conducting independent analysis into climate change science, economics and policy
- Engaging with a wide range of organisations and individuals to share evidence and analysis.

The CCC has eight members in total and the adaptation subcommittee has six. With the exception of the chair, who is a high-profile politicians, most members are technical experts who are chosen and appointed by national authorities on the basis of their specialised knowledge and experience. Each member has a fixed term appointment of five years, with the possibility of reappointment. Like its equivalents in the EU, the CCC is primarily an advisory body, and it has no formal decision-making or legal enforcement powers. However, it produces a detailed annual report on the UK's progress at tackling climate change to Parliament, to which the government has a statutory obligation to respond (UK Government, 2008).

Fankhauser, Averchenkova and Finnegan (2018) find that CCC has made a notable difference to UK climate policy since its establishment and helped push for greater ambition with regard to both mitigation and adaptation. However, more recently, the gap between committee recommendations and actual policy appears to have widened. In its 2019 progress report, the CCC revealed that only one of the twenty-five headline policy actions it had recommended in its previous report had been fully delivered, with ten not even showing partial progress. It also noted that this lack of action has led to the UK being off track for achieving its fourth and fifth carbon budgets (CCC, 2019).

7 Conclusion: What Does the Future Hold for Global Climate Change Governance?

Whether or not existing global climate governance configurations can be repurposed to deliver the rapid and far-reaching measures required to prevent catastrophic global warming remains an open question. The Paris Agreement may have saved the chance to save the planet, but the window for preventive mitigation action is closing. Without global system-wide decarbonization measures, scientific studies predict that global temperatures will cross the 2 °C warming threshold as soon as 2035 (Aengenheyster et al., 2018). This risk imperative is informing policymaking at the highest levels, as well as mobilizing civil society to demand action. This Element has presented an overview summary of the state of global climate change governance in 2020. It highlights above all the incredible diversity of state and non-state actors, as well as the huge potential for positive innovation upon existing governance structures, beyond top-down regulation. Nevertheless, climate governance scholars predict a rocky road ahead, observing a move from conventional distributional politics (who gets what, when and how) to existential politics which 'is like distributional politics on steroids: the stakes are whose way of life gets to survive' (Green, Hale and Colgan, 2019).

Cooperation problems continue to stymie effective global climate governance. The political leadership that enabled the adoption of the Paris Agreement in 2015 has since then dissipated. The two most recent COPs saw a number of powerful states actively blocking progress or staying at the sidelines, undermining momentum for the scaling up of collective and individual ambition. The Paris rulebook is still not fully finalized after governments proved unable to agree on a robust framework for the Agreement's market mechanisms at COP-25 in Madrid. Even the scientific basis for greater ambition has become a matter of contestation again, with the United States and other oil- and gas-producing countries refusing to 'welcome' the IPCC's special report on global warming of

1.5 °C. Meanwhile, coordination problems have, if anything, intensified as existing global governance structures struggle to manage interface conflict and effectively exploit potential synergies between climate change and other governance domains. Indeed, we may no longer have the time to carefully 'manage' such relationships, given that climate change and the threat of ecological breakdown require prioritization over less existential and/or less urgent risks (Cashore and Bernstein, 2020). However, in a global economy that still runs overwhelmingly on fossil fuels, powerful states and vested private interests will continue to challenge efforts to fundamentally disrupt carbon lock-in (IEA, 2020). Going forward, such efforts will also have to increasingly contend with the 'imperatives of a just transition' (UNFCCC, 2015); the need to secure broad-based societal buy-in by sharing the costs and benefits of ambitious climate action in a fair and equitable manner on the global, national and local level. Indeed, as Aklin and Mildenberger (2018) argue, entrenched distributive conflict on the domestic level may be one of the primary obstacles to effective global climate governance.

The COVID-19 pandemic has generated both challenges and opportunities for future climate governance. While lockdowns and other response measure have temporarily resulted in a sharp drop of GHG emissions, the overall effect on global warming will be 'close to negligible' (Forster et al., 2020: 6). Much will depend on whether economic recovery choices reflect a commitment to pursue deep and long-term structural change (Allan et al., 2020). In terms of global governance, COVID-19 serves as a sobering warning that encouraging collective action does not get easier in the face of acute crisis. Given its lack of resources and independent authority, the World Health Organization (WHO) has struggled to coordinate an effective response (Pegram, 2020). Even relatively 'technical' decisions, such as the formal declaration of COVID-19 as a Public Health Emergency of International Concern, have become highly politicized (Borger, 2020). Powerful states, notably China and the United States, have been accused of delaying the release of vital data (Kuo, 2020) or even engaging in 'modern piracy' to secure protective gear (Willsher, Borger and Holmes, 2020). Currently, these states also appear unlikely to prioritize decarbonization in their COVID-19 recovery strategies (Farand, 2020).

Beyond the need for global coordination and cooperation, COVID-19 has demonstrated the enduring relevance of national and local institutional capacity for the effective response to global risks (Pegram, 2020). As this volume in the Elements series has sought to convey, the transmission of global policy standards and their effective enabling within domestic political systems are a crucial component of global (climate) governance structures and processes. The Paris Agreement represents a paradigmatic operational shift towards global-to-local policy implementation, with potential application to other policy domains. It also has implications for major debates in global governance, public policy and international law, focused on advancing a research and policy agenda which moves the debate beyond questions of IGO institutional design to enabling evidence-based policymaking and community action on the part of local governance participants. The ambitious climate targets set by the Paris Agreement demand rapid (re)deployment of local institutional capacity and public buy-in. Empowered, independent climate advisory bodies and MRV agencies promise to be a central pillar of this new phase of climate governance.

Scholars of multi-level governance, global regulation and public policy have much to gain from assessing the promise of this emerging multi-scalar climate regulatory apparatus, as well as probing the post-delegation risks posed by such policy transfers absent clear international coordination frameworks, as well as, and crucially, the implementation challenge in settings of divergent national preferences and uneven institutional capacity (Thatcher and Coen, 2008). Pioneering policy-applied research by Victor, Geels and Sharpe (2019: 105), among others, highlights one promising line of inquiry into the crucial role of experimentalist learning, coordinated diffusion and a contracting approach to 'lock new [desirable] practices into place' and 'accelerate emergence' in multi-level governance systems. Frontier scholarship is also clarifying the 'wickedly hard problem' posed by entrenched systemic drivers of climate change, the 'overlapping and interdependent political, economic, technological and cultural forces that reinforce dependence on fossil fuels in many places simultaneously' (Bernstein and Hoffmann, 2019: 919). Balancing a pragmatic concern for problem-solving with a critical appraisal of structural power in light of the evident complexity of human and social systems will be a daunting, but vital, endeavour for future theoretical and empirical research on global climate governance.

Glossary of Key Acronyms and Abbreviations

CBDR-RC: Common but Differentiated Responsibilities and Respective Capabilities, a principle enshrined in the 1992 United Nations Framework Convention on Climate Change, acknowledging that, while all state parties have an obligation to address climate change, some have more capability and a greater responsibility to do so than others

CCC: Committee on Climate Change, an independent expert body established under the United Kingdom's 2008 Climate Change Act to advise on implementation of the Act and monitor progress made towards its goals

CDM: Clean Development Mechanism, a market mechanism established through the 1997 Kyoto Protocol allowing developed countries to earn credits towards their own mitigation targets through the implementation of emissions reduction projects in developing countries

CMA: Conference of the Parties serving as the meeting of the Parties to the Paris Agreement, the supreme decision-making body for the Paris Agreement

CMP: Conference of the Parties serving as the meeting of the Parties to the Kyoto Protocol, the supreme decision-making body for the Kyoto Protocol

Convention: 1992 United Nations Framework Convention on Climate Change

COP: Conference of the Parties, the supreme decision-making body of the United Nations Framework Convention on Climate Change. Annual United Nations climate change conferences are often simply referred to as the

	'COP', however, they are held in conjunction with sessions of the CMP and CMA (the supreme decision-making bodies of the Kyoto Protocol and the Paris Agreement). For example, the 2019 meeting in Madrid was officially known as 'COP 25 / CMP 15 / CMA 2'
DG CLIMA:	Directorate-General for Climate Action, European Commission department dedicated to climate change
ETF:	Enhanced Transparency Framework, a key component of the Paris Agreement, requiring all state parties to report biannually on progress made towards implementation of their national climate targets under a common set of guidelines and subject to expert and peer review
EU:	European Union
EU-ETS:	The European Union's Emissions Trading System
GCAA:	Global Climate Action Agenda, officially launched in 2016 but building on earlier efforts under the Lima–Paris Action Agenda (LPAA), aims to galvanize climate action by a broad array of non-state actors
GEF:	Global Environment Facility, a global partnership that serves as a major financing mechanism for the protection of the environment, including as an operating entity of the financial mechanism of the UNFCCC
GHG:	Greenhouse gas, a gas that absorbs infrared radiation emitted from the Earth's surface and re-emits it back the earth, thus contributing to the warming of the lower atmosphere
GPG:	Global public good, a good whose benefits and costs extend to many (potentially all) countries, populations and generations
IGO:	Intergovernmental organization
IIGO:	Informal intergovernmental organization, not operating on the basis of a formal, legal

	treaty but with a relatively permanent membership, consisting primarily of sovereign states
IPCC:	Intergovernmental Panel on Climate Change, a United Nations body dedicated to providing regular scientific assessments on climate change and its impact as well as options for mitigation and adaptation
L&D:	Loss and damage, 'residual' impacts of climate change that can no longer be prevented or effectively alleviated through adaptation
LPAA:	Lima–Paris Action Agenda, launched in 2014 by the governments of France and Peru, the UN Secretary General and UNFCCC Secretariat with the aim of bringing together a broad coalition of state and non-state stakeholders to encourage ambitious climate action. Since 2016, this effort has been continued through the Global Climate Action Agenda (GCAA)
MEF:	Major Economies Forum on Energy and Climate, launched in 2009 by then US President Barack Obama, with the aim of catalyzing action and facilitating dialogue on climate change among seventeen major emitters (now largely inactive)
MRV:	Monitoring, Reporting and Verification, the process of transparently tracking emissions, climate policies and/or climate finance, on the national, subnational, sectoral or project level
NAZCA:	Non-state Actor Zone for Climate Action, an online portal hosted by the UNFCCC that highlights actions taken by cities, regions, companies and investors to address climate change
NDC:	Nationally Determined Contribution, national climate pledge submitted under the Paris Agreement
NGO:	Non-governmental organization

PPP: Public–private partnership, a voluntary and relatively long-term cooperative arrangement between public actors (e.g. international organizations, states or public authorities) and non-state actors (e.g. NGOs, foundations, companies or investors) with the aim of delivering (global) public goods and/or services

UN: United Nations

UNEP or UN Environment: United Nations Environment Programme, now rebranded UN Environment, coordinates environmental activities within the United Nations system

UNFCCC: United Nations Framework Convention on Climate Change, may refer to both the Convention and the broader institutional framework facilitating its implementation

WIM: Warsaw Mechanism on Loss and Damage, dedicated UNFCCC mechanism to address the residual impacts of climate change

Bibliography

Abbott, K. W. (2012). The transnational regime complex for climate change. *Environment and Planning C: Government and Policy*, 30(4),571–90.

Acuto, M. (2013). *Global Cities, Governance and Diplomacy. The Urban Link*. London: Routledge.

Acuto, M., and Rayner, S. (2016). City networks: breaking gridlocks or forging (new) lock-ins? *International Affairs*, 92(5),1147–66.

Adaptation Fund (n.d.). Website of the Adaptation Fund [online]. www.adapta tion-fund.org/.

Aengenheyster, M., Feng, Q. Y., van der Ploeg, F., and Dijkstra, H. A. (2018). The point of no return for climate action: effects of climate uncertainty and risk tolerance. *Earth System Dynamics*, 9, 1085–95.

Agrawala, S. (1998). Structural and process history of the Intergovernmental Panel on Climate Change. *Climatic Change*, 39(4),621–42.

Aklin, M., and Mildenberger, M. (2018). 'Prisoners of the wrong dilemma: why distributive conflict, not collective action, characterizes the politics of climate change.' *SSRN Working Paper* [online]. https://papers.ssrn.com/sol3/papers.cfm?abstract_id=3281045.

Allan, J., et al. (2020). A net-zero emissions economic recovery from COVID-19. *SSEE Working Paper*, No. 20–01. Oxford Smith School of Enterprise and the Environment [online]. 4 May 2020. www.smithschool.ox.ac.uk/publica tions/wpapers/workingpaper20-01.pdf.

Alter, K. J, . and Raustiala, K. (2018). The rise of international regime complexity. *Annual Review of Law and Social Science*, 14, 329–49.

Andonova, L. B. (2017). *Governance Entrepreneurs: International Organizations and the Rise of Global Public-Private Partnerships*. Cambridge: Cambridge University Press.

Andonova, L. B., and Levy, M. A. (2003). Franchising global governance: Making sense of the Johannesburg type II partnerships. In O. S. Stokke and O. Thommessen, eds., *Yearbook of International Co-operation on Environment and Development 2003/2004*. London: Earthscan, 19–31.

Antonich, B. (2019). Number of climate adaptation projects increases, so must their quality. *SDG Knowledge Hub* [online]. 21 March 2019. International Institute for Sustainable Development (IISD). https://sdg.iisd.org/news/adap tation-finance-update-number-of-climate-adaptation-projects-increases-so-must-their-quality/.

Appleby, K. (2019). What the 1.5°C-degree report means for city climate action. CDP Blog [online]. 18 September 2019. www.cdp.net/en/articles/ cities/what-the-15 c-degree-report-means-for-city-climate-action.

Arroyo, V. (2018). The global climate action summit: increasing ambition during turbulent times. *Climate Policy*, 18(9),1087–93.

Averchenkova, A. (2019). *Legislating for a low carbon and climate resilient transition: learning from international experiences*. Elcano Policy Paper [online]. January 2019. Madrid: Real Instituto Elcano. www.realinstitutoel cano.org/wps/wcm/connect/130a3d55-dd9f-4ce1-ac04-a3caf5910edf/ Policy-Paper-2019-Legislating-low-carbon-climate-resilient-transition.pdf? MOD=AJPERES&CACHEID=130a3d55-dd9 f-4ce1-ac04-a3caf5910edf.

Averchenkova, A., Fankhauser, S., and Finnegan, J. (2018). The role of independent bodies in climate governance: the UK's Committee on Climate Change [online]. October 2018. London: The Grantham Research Institute on Climate Change and the Environment and Centre for Climate Change Economics and Policy, London School of Economics and Political Science. www.lse.ac.uk/GranthamInstitute/wp-content/uploads/2018/10/The-role-of-independent-bodies-in-climate-governance-the-UKs-Committee-on-Climate-Change_Averchenkova-et-al.pdf.

Ayers, J. (2011). Resolving the adaptation paradox: exploring the potential for deliberative adaptation policy-making in Bangladesh. *Global Environmental Politics*, 11(1),62–88.

Bäckstrand, K. (2008). Accountability of networked climate governance: the rise of transnational climate partnerships. *Global Environmental Politics*, 8(3),74–102.

Bäckstrand, K., and Elgström, O. (2013). The EU's role in climate change negotiations: from leader to 'leadiator'. *Journal of European Public Policy*, 20(10),1369–86.

Bäckstrand, K., and Kuyper, J. W. (2017). The democratic legitimacy of orchestration: the UNFCCC, non-state actors, and transnational climate governance. *Environmental Politics*, 26(4),764–88.

Bäckstrand, K., Kuyper, J. W., Linnér, B. O., and Lövbrand, E. (2017). Non-state actors in global climate governance: from Copenhagen to Paris and beyond. *Environmental Politics*, 26(4),561–79.

Bäckstrand, K., and Lövbrand, E. (2016). The road to Paris: contending climate governance discourses in the post-Copenhagen era. *Journal of Environmental Policy & Planning*, 18, 1–19.

Barnard, A. (2019). A 'Climate Emergency' was declared in New York City. Will that change anything? *The New York Times* [online]. 5 July 2019. www .nytimes.com/2019/07/05/nyregion/climate-emergency-nyc.html.

Barrett, S. (2007). *Why Cooperate? The Incentive to Supply Global Public Goods*. Oxford: Oxford University Press.

Basu, J. (2019). Climate Emergency CoP 25: loss and damage 'fighting out' in Madrid. *DownToEarth* [online]. 13 December 2019. www.downtoearth.org .in/news/climate-change/climate-emergency-cop-25-loss-and-damage-fight ing-out-in-madrid-68416.

Baur, D., and Schmitz, H. P. (2012). Corporations and NGOs: when accountability leads to co-optation. *Journal of Business Ethics*, 106(1),9–21.

Beck, S. (2012). Between tribalism and trust: the IPCC under the 'public microscope'. *Nature and Culture*, 7(2),151–73.

Beck, S., and Mahony, M. (2018). The IPCC and the new map of science and politics. *WIREs Climate Change*, 9(6),e547, 1–16.

Benvenisti, E., and Downs, G.W. (2007). The empire's new clothes: political economy and the fragmentation of international law. *Stanford Law Review*, 60(2),595–631.

Benson, D., and Lorenzoni, I. (2014). Examining the scope for national lesson-drawing on climate governance. *Political Quarterly*, 85(2),202–11.

Benzie, M., et al. (2018). Meeting the global challenge of adaptation by addressing transboundary climate risk. Discussion Brief. Stockholm Environment Institute [online]. www.sei.org/wp-content/uploads/2018/04/ meetingtheglobalchallengeofadaptation.pdf.

Berg, M., and Lidskog, R. (2018). Pathways to deliberative capacity: the role of the IPCC. *Climatic Change*, 148(1–2), 11–24.

Berglund, N. (2018). Solheim resigns as UN climate chief. *News in English Norway* [online]. 20 November 2018. www.newsinenglish.no/2018/11/20/ solheim-resigns-as-un-climate-chief/.

Berliner, D., and Prakash, A. (2015). 'Bluewashing' the firm? voluntary regulations, program design, and member compliance with the United Nations Global Compact. *Policy Studies Journal*, 43(1),115–38.

Bernstein, S., and Hoffman, M. (2018). The politics of decarbonization and the catalytic impact of subnational climate experiments. *Policy Science*, 51, 189–211.

Bernstein S., and Hoffmann, M. (2019). Climate politics, metaphors and the fractal carbon trap. *Nature Climate Change*, 9, 919–25.

Berny, N., and Rootes, C. (2018). Environmental NGOs at a crossroads? *Environmental Politics*, 27(6), 947–72.

Berwyn, B. (2020). Coronavirus already hindering climate science, but the worst disruptions are likely yet to come. *Inside Climate News* [online]. 27 March 2020. https://insideclimatenews.org/news/26032020/coronavirus-climate-science-research-impact.

Betsill, M. M. (2007). Regional governance of global climate change: the North American Commission for Environmental Cooperation. *Global Environmental Politics*, 7(2),11–27.

Betsill, M. M., and Bulkeley, H. (2006). Cities and the multilevel governance of global climate change. *Global Governance*, 12(2),141–59.

Bexell, M., and Mörth, U. (2010). Introduction: Partnerships, democracy and governance. In M. Bexell and U. Mörth, eds., *Democracy and Public-Private Partnerships in Global Governance*. Baskingstoke: Palgrave Macmillan, 3–23.

Biermann, F. and Boas, I. (2010). Global adaptation governance: setting the stage. In F. Biermann, P. Pattberg and F. Zelli, eds., *Global Climate Governance beyond 2012: Architecture, Agency and Adaptation*. New York, NY: Cambridge University Press, 223–34.

Biermann, F., Pattberg, P., van Asselt, H., and Zelli, F. (2009). The fragmentation of global governance architectures: a framework for analysis. *Global Environmental Politics*, 9(4),14–40.

Blackstock, J. J., et al. (2009). *Climate Engineering Responses to Climate Emergencies*. Santa Barbara, CA: Novim [online]. 29 July 2009. https://arxiv.org/ftp/arxiv/papers/0907/0907.5140.pdf.

Bodansky, D. (2016). The Paris Agreement: a new hope? *The American Journal of International Law*, 110(2),288–319.

Bodansky, D., Brunnée, J., and Rajamani, L. (2017). *International Climate Change Law*. Oxford: Oxford University Press.

Bodansky, D. (2015). Reflections on the Paris conference. *Opinio Juris* [online]. 15 December 2015. http://opiniojuris.org/2015/12/15/reflections-on-the-paris-conference/.

Bocse, A.-M. (2019). The UK's decision to leave the European Union (Brexit) and its impact on the EU as a climate change actor. *Climate Policy*, 1–11.

Borger, J. (2020). Caught in a superpower struggle: the inside story of the WHO's response to coronavirus. *The Guardian* [online]. 18 April 2020. www.theguardian.com/world/2020/apr/18/caught-in-a-superpower-struggle-the-inside-story-of-the-whos-response-to-coronavirus.

Bouteligier, S. (2012). Inequality in new global governance arrangements: the North–South divide in transnational municipal networks. *Innovation: The European Journal of Social Science Research*, 26(3),251–67.

Broberg, M. (2020). Interpreting the UNFCCC's provisions on 'mitigation' and 'adaptation' in light of the Paris Agreement's provision on 'loss and damage'. *Climate Policy*, 20(5),527–33.

Brown, L. D., Ebrahim, A., and Batliwala, S. (2012). Governing international advocacy NGOs. *World Development*, 40(6),1098–108.

Brown, K., Adger, W. N., and Cinner, J. E. (2019). Moving climate change beyond the tragedy of the commons. *Global Environmental Change*, 54, 61–3.

Brunnée, J., Doelle, M., and Rajamani, L. (2011). *Promoting Compliance in an Evolving Climate Regime*. Cambridge: Cambridge University Press.

Bulkeley, H., et al. (2014). *Transnational Climate Change Governance*. Cambridge: Cambridge University Press.

Busby, J., and Hadden, J. (2014), *Nonstate actors in the climate arena* [online]. 19 November 2014. Sponsored by The Stanley Foundation, National Defense University, and World Future Society. www.stanleyfoundation.org/publica tions/working_papers/StanleyNonState_BusbyHadden.pdf.

Busch, P.-O. (2009). The Climate Secretariat: making a living in a straitjacket. In F. Biermann and B. Siebenhüner, eds., *Managers of Global Change: The Influence of International Environmental Bureaucracies*. Cambridge, MA: MIT Press, 245–64.

Calliari, E., Surminski, S. and Mysiak, J. (2019). The politics of (and behind) the UNFCCC's Loss and Damage Mechanism. In R. Mechler et al., eds., *Loss and Damage from Climate Change: Concepts, Methods and Policy Options*. Cham: Springer, 155–78.

Carbon Brief (2018). COP-24: Key outcomes agreed at the UN climate talks in Katowice [online]. 16 December 2018. www.carbonbrief.org/COP-24-key-outcomes-agreed-at-the-un-climate-talks-in-katowice.

Carrington, D. (2011). Q&A: 'Climategate'. *The Guardian* [online]. 22 November 2011. www.theguardian.com/environment/2010/jul/07/cli mate-emails-question-answer.

Cashore, B., and Bernstein, S. (2020). Bringing the environment back in: overcoming the tragedy of the diffusion of the commons metaphor. Substantially revised version of papers presented to the Ostrom Workshop at Indiana University, 23 April 23 2018, Bloomington, Indiana and the International Studies Association Annual Meeting, San Francisco, 3–7 April 2018.

CCAC (n.d.). Terms of membership. Irish Climate Change Advisory Council (CCAC) [online]. www.climatecouncil.ie/aboutus/councilmembers/termsof councilmembership/.

CCC (2019). *Summary Report. 2019 Progress Report to Parliament* [online]. July 2019. UK Committee on Climate Change. www.theccc.org.uk/wp-con tent/uploads/2019/07/2019-Progress-Report-Summary.pdf.

CDP (n.d.) CDP website [online]. www.cdp.net/en.

CEO (2019). Big Oil and Gas spent over 250 million euros lobbying the EU. Brussels: Corporate Europe Observatory (CEO) [online]. 23 October 2019.

https://corporateeurope.org/en/2019/10/big-oil-and-gas-spent-over-250-mil
lion-euros-lobbying-eu.

Challies, E. and Newig, J. (2019). What is 'environmental governance'?
A working definition. Sustainability Governance [online]. https://sustainabil
ity-governance.net/2019/06/14/what-is-environmental-governance-a-work
ing-definition/.

Chan, S., and Amling, W. (2019). Does orchestration in the Global Climate
Action Agenda effectively prioritize and mobilize transnational climate
adaptation action? *International Environmental Agreements: Politics, Law
and Economics*, 19(4–5), 429–46.

Chan, S., et al. (2015). Reinvigorating international climate policy:
a comprehensive framework for effective nonstate action. *Global Policy*, 6
(4),466–73.

Chan, S., et al. (2018). *Cooperative Climate Action: Global Performance &
Delivery in the Global South*. Research report published by the African
Centre for Technology Studies (ACTS), the Blavatnik School of Government
and Global Economic Governance Programme at the University of Oxford, the
German Development Institute/Deutsches Institut für Entwicklungspolitik
(DIE) and TERI University [online]. www.geg.ox.ac.uk/sites/geg.bsg.ox.ac
.uk/files/2018–11/ClimateSouth%20-%20GCAS%20Brief.pdf.

Chan, S., Brandi, C., and Bauer, S. (2016). Aligning transnational climate action
with international climate governance: the road from Paris. *RECIEL*, 25
(2),238–47.

Christoff, P. (2016). The promissory note: COP 21 and the Paris Climate
Agreement. *Environmental Politics*, 25(5),765–87.

CIEL (2019). It's a crisis; act like it: COP-25 outcome inconsistent with urgency
and ambition demanded to confront the climate crisis. Center for
International Environmental Law [online]. www.ciel.org/news/its-a-crisis-
act-like-it-COP-25-outcome-inconsistent-with-urgency-and-ambition-
demanded-to-confront-the-climate-crisis/.

Ciplet, D., Roberts, J. T., and Khan, M. (2013). The politics of international
climate adaptation funding: justice and divisions in the greenhouse. *Global
Environmental Politics*, 13(1),49–68.

Climate Action Tracker (2019). Warming projections. Global Update [online].
September 2019. https://climateactiontracker.org/documents/644/CAT_2019–
09-19_BriefingUNSG_WarmingProjectionsGlobalUpdate_Sept2019.pdf.

Climate Action Tracker (n.d.). EU Profile [online]. https://climateactiontracker
.org/countries/eu/.

Coen, D., and Pegram, T. (2018). Towards a third generation of global governance scholarship. *Global Policy*, 9(1),107–13.

Cogswell, N., and Dagnet, Y. (2019). *Why does the Paris Climate Agreement need a rulebook? 7 questions and answers.* World Resources Institute (WRI) [online]. www.wri.org/blog/2019/06/why-does-paris-climate-agreement-need-rulebook-7-questions-and-answers.

Cole, D. H. (2015). Shared irresponsibilities in international climate law. In A. Nollkaemper and D. Jacobs, eds., *Distribution of Responsibilities in International Law.* Cambridge: Cambridge University Press, 290–320.

Conca, K. (2018). Is there a role for the UN Security Council on Climate Change? *Environment: Science and Policy for Sustainable Development,* 61(1),4–15.

Corbera, E., Calvet-Mir, L., Hughes, H., and Paterson, M. (2016). Patterns of authorship in the IPCC Working Group III report. *Nature Climate Change,* 6, 94–99.

Council of the European Union (n.d.). Environment Council configuration (ENVI) [online]. www.consilium.europa.eu/en/council-eu/configurations/env/.

Curtis, S. (2014). *The Power of Cities in International Relations.* New York: Routledge.

Das, K., van Asselt, H., Droege, S., and Mehling, M. (2018). Making the international trade system work for climate change: assessing the options. Climate Strategies [online]. https://climatestrategies.org/wp-content/uploads/2018/07/CS-Report-_Trade-WP4.pdf.

Delbeke, J., and Vis, P. (2016). EU climate policy explained. European Union [online]. https://ec.europa.eu/clima/sites/clima/files/eu_climate_policy_ex plained_en.pdf.

Doelle, M. (2016). The Paris Agreement: historic breakthrough or high stakes experiment? *Climate Law,* 6(1–2),1–20.

Drexhage, J. (2008). Climate change and global governance: which way ahead? *Global Environmental Governance (GEG) Briefing Paper,* No. 2. International Institute for Sustainable Development (IISD) [online]. April 2008. www.iisd .org/pdf/2008/geg_climate_gov.pdf.

Drezner, D. W. (2009). The power and peril of international regime complexity. *Perspectives on Politics,* 7(1),65–70.

Duggan, J. (2019). *The role of sub-state and non-state actors in international climate processes: subnational governments* [online]. Background Paper, January 2019. London: Chatham House. www.chathamhouse.org/sites/default/files/publications/2019–01-23-Duggan.pdf.

Dunne, D. (2018). Explainer: Ssx ideas to limit global warming with solar geoengineering. *CarbonBrief* [online]. 9 May 2018. www.carbonbrief.org/explainer-six-ideas-to-limit-global-warming-with-solar-geoengineering.

Duwe, M. et al. (2017). *'Paris compatible' governance: long-term policy frameworks to drive transformational change.* Ecologic Institute [online]. www.ecologic.eu/sites/files/publication/2018/2138-governance-to-fight-climate-change-112018_0.pdf.

Dyck, S. (2017). The Paris climate agreement and the protection of human rights in a changing climate. *Yearbook of International Environmental Law*, 26, 3–45.

E360 (2015). Five questions for Bill McKibben on the Paris Climate Agreement. *Yale Environment 360* [online]. 16 December 2015. https://e360.yale.edu/digest/five_questions_for_bill_mckibben_on_the_paris_climate_agreement.

ETC Group (2009). The Emperor's new climate: geoengineering as 21st century fairytale. ETC Group Special Report [online]. 28 August 2009. www.etcgroup.org/sites/www.etcgroup.org/files/publication/pdf_file/etcspecialreport_rsgeoeng28aug09.pdf.

Esty, D. C. (2009). Revitalizing global environmental governance for climate change. *Global Governance*, 15(4),427–434.

European Commission (2018). EU-China leaders' statement on climate change and clean energy [online]. Beijing, 16 July 2018. https://ec.europa.eu/clima/sites/clima/files/news/20180713_statement_en.pdf.

European Commission (2019). Ready, Steady, Green! LIFE helps farming and forestry adapt to climate change [online]. Luxembourg: Publications Office of the European Union. https://op.europa.eu/en/publication-detail/-/publication/8119493 f-db52-11e9-9c4e-01aa75ed71a1/language-en/format-PDF/source-106529364.

European Commission (n.d.a). 2050 long-term strategy [online]. https://ec.europa.eu/clima/policies/strategies/2050_en.

European Commission (n.d.b). A European Green Deal [online]. https://ec.europa.eu/info/strategy/priorities-2019–2024/european-green-deal_en

European Commission (n.d.c). Directorate-General for Climate Action (DG CLIMA) – What we do [online]. https://ec.europa.eu/clima/about-us/mission_en.

European Commission (n.d.d). National energy and climate plans (NECPs) [online]. https://ec.europa.eu/info/energy-climate-change-environment/overall-targets/national-energy-and-climate-plans-necps_en.

European Commission (n.d.e.). Emissions monitoring & reporting [online]. https://ec.europa.eu/clima/policies/strategies/progress/monitoring_en.

European Environment Agency (2019). *Annual European Union greenhouse gas inventory 1990–2017 and the inventory report 2019.* Submission under the United Nations Framework Convention on Climate Change and the Kyoto Protocol. 27 May 2019. EEA/PUBL/2019/051.

Fahys, J. (2020). In the face of a pandemic, climate activists reevaluate their tactics. *Inside Climate News* [online]. 20 March 2020. https://insideclimate news.org/news/19032020/climate-change-activism-coronavirus.

Falkner, R. (2016a). The Paris Agreement and the new logic of international climate politics. *International Affairs*, 92(5),1107–1125.

Falkner, R. (2016b). A minilateral solution for global climate change? on bargaining efficiency, club benefits, and international legitimacy. *Perspectives on Politics*, 14(1),87–101.

Falkner, R. (2010). Business and global climate governance: a neo-pluralist perspective. In M. Ougaard and A. Leander, eds., *Business and Global Governance*. London: Routledge, 99–117.

Falkner, R., Stephan, H. and Vogler, J. (2010). International climate policy after Copenhagen: towards a 'building blocks' approach. *Global Policy*, 1(3),252–62.

Fankhauser, S., Averchenkova, A. and Finnegan, J. (2018). 10 years of the UK Climate Change Act. London: The Grantham Research Institute on Climate Change and the Environment and the Centre for Climate Change Economics and Policy. London School of Economics and Political Science [online]. www.lse.ac.uk/GranthamInstitute/wp-content/uploads/2018/03/10-Years-of-the-UK-Climate-Change-Act_Fankhauser-et-al.pdf.

Farand, C. (2019). The UN asked for climate plans. Major economies failed to answer. *Climate Home News* [online]. 24 September 2019. www.climate changenews.com/2019/09/24/un-asked-climate-plans-major-economies-failed-answer/.

Farand, C. (2020). Guterres confronts China over coal boom, urging a green recovery. Climate Home News [online]. 23 July 2020. www.climatechange news.com/2020/07/23/guterres-confronts-china-coal-boom-urging-green-recovery/.

Fehl, C., and Thimm, J. (2019). Dispensing with the indispensable nation? multilateralism minus one in the Trump era. *Global Governance: A Review of Multilateralism and International Organizations*, 25(1),23–46.

Finck, M. (2014). Above and below the surface: the status of sub-national authorities in EU climate change regulation. *Journal of Environmental Law*, 26(3),443–72.

Forster, P. M., et al. (2020). Current and future global climate impacts resulting from COVID-19. *Nature Climate Change*, 1–15.

G7 Information Centre (n.d.). Declaration of the 1979 G7 Summit [online]. Tokyo, 29 June 1979. www.g7.utoronto.ca/summit/1979tokyo/communique.html.

G20 (2019). Safeguarding the planet [online]. https://g20.org/en/Documents/Safeguarding%20the%20Planet.pdf

Garrelts, H., and Dietz, M. (2013). Introduction. In M. Dietz and H. Garrelts, eds., *Routledge Handbook of the Climate Change Movement*. New York: Routledge, 1–15.

Gehring, T., and Faude, B. (2013). The dynamics of regime complexes: micro-foundations and systemic effects. *Global Governance*, 19(1),119–30.

Gereke, M., and Brühl, T. (2019). Unpacking the unequal representation of Northern and Southern NGOs in international climate change politics. *Third World Quarterly*, 40(5),870–89.

GGI (2018). Towards a third generation of global governance scholarship. The Global Governance Institute [online]. 21 May 2018. London: University College London. www.ucl.ac.uk/global-governance/news/2018/may/towards-third-generation-global-governance-scholarship.

Gill, S. (2012). Organic crisis, global leadership and progressive alternatives. In S. Gill, ed., *Global Crises and the Crisis of Global Leadership*. Cambridge: Cambridge University Press, 233–54.

Gollier, C., and Tirole, J. (2015). Negotiating effective institutions against climate change. *Economics of Energy & Environmental Policy*, 4(2),5–28.

Graham, E. R., and Thompson, A. (2015). Efficient orchestration? the global environment facility in the governance of climate adaptation. In K. W. Abott, P. Genschel, D. Snidal and B. Zangl, eds., *International Organizations as Orchestrators*. Cambridge: Cambridge University Press, 114–38.

Grasso, M., and Roberts, J. T. (2014). A compromise to break the climate impasse. *Nature Climate Change*, 4, 543–9.

Grasso, M., and Vladimirova, K. (2020). A moral analysis of carbon majors' role in climate change. *Environmental Values*, 29(2),175–95.

Gray, B., and Purdy, J. (2018). *Collaborating for Our Future: Multistakeholder Partnerships for Solving Complex Problems*. Oxford: Oxford University Press.

Green Climate Fund (n.d.). Website of the Green Climate Fund [online]. www.greenclimate.fund/home.

Green, J. (2010). Private standards in the climate regime: the Greenhouse Gas Protocol. *Business and Politics*, 12(3),1–37.

Green, J. (2014). *Rethinking Private Authority: Agents and Entrepreneurs in Global Environmental Governance*. Princeton, NJ: Princeton University Press.

Green, J. (2017). Don't link carbon markets. *Nature*, 543, 484–6.

Green, J., Hale, T., and Colgan, J. D. (2019). The existential politics of climate change. *Global Policy Blog* [online]. 21 February 2019. www.globalpolicyjournal.com/blog/21/02/2019/existential-politics-climate-change.

Grubb, M. (2016). Why it's wrong to label the Kyoto Protocol a disaster. *Climate Home News* [online]. 10 June 2016. www.climatechangenews.com/2016/06/10/why-its-wrong-to-label-the-kyoto-protocol-a-disaster/.

Gupta, A., and Mason, M. (2016). Disclosing or obscuring? the politics of transparency in climate governance. *Current Opinion in Environmental Sustainability*, 18, 82–90.

Haas, P. M., and Stevens, C. (2011). Organized science, usable knowledge, and multilateral environmental governance. In R. Lidskog and G. Sundqvist, eds., *Governing the Air: The Dynamics of Science, Policy, and Citizen Interaction.* Cambridge, MA: MIT Press, 125–62.

Haass, R. (2020). The pandemic will accelerate history rather than reshape it. *Foreign Affairs* [online]. 7 April 2020. www.foreignaffairs.com/articles/united-states/2020–04-07/pandemic-will-accelerate-history-rather-reshape-it.

Hale, T. (2016). 'All hands on deck': The Paris Agreement and nonstate climate action. *Global Environmental Politics*, 16(3),12–22.

Hale, T. (2017). Climate change: from gridlock to catalyst. In T. Hale and D. Held, eds., *Beyond Gridlock.* Cambridge: Polity Press, 184–204.

Hale, T. (2019). UN climate talks must include cities, businesses or risk irrelevance. *Climate Home News* [online]. 9 October 2019. www.climatechangenews.com/2019/10/09/un-climate-talks-must-include-cities-businesses-risk-irrelevance/.

Hall, N., and Persson, Å. (2018). Global climate adaptation governance: why is it not legally binding? *European Journal of International Relations*, 24 (3),540–66.

Harari, Y. N. (2017). Nationalism vs. globalism: the new political divide. TED Dialogues [online video]. February 2017. www.ted.com/talks/yuval_noah_harari_nationalism_vs_globalism_the_new_political_divide.

Harrison, N. E., and Geyer, R. (2019). The complexity of the governance of climate change. In A. Orsini et al., Forum: Complex Systems and International Governance. *International Studies Review*, 0, 21–4.

Haufler, V. (2018). Producing global governance in the global factory: markets, politics, and regulation. *Global Policy*, 9(1),114–20.

Held, D., and Roger, C. (2018). Three models of global climate governance: From Kyoto to Paris and beyond. *Global Policy*, 9(4),527–37.

Helmore, E. (2019). Wall Street investment giants voting against key climate resolutions. *The Guardian* [online]. 17 September 2019. www.theguardian.com/environment/2019/sep/17/wall-street-asset-management-climate-change-blackrock-vanguard.

Hermwille, L. (2018). Making initiatives resonate: how can non-state initiatives advance national contributions under the UNFCCC? *International Environmental Agreements: Politics, Law and Economics*, 18(3),447–66.

Hermwille, L., Obergassel, W., Ott, H. E., and Beuermann, C. (2017). UNFCCC before and after Paris: what's necessary for an effective climate regime? *Climate Policy*, 17(2),150–70.

Hickmann, T. (2017). The reconfiguration of authority in global climate governance. *International Studies Review*, 19(3),430–51.

Hickmann, T., Widerberg, O., Lederer, M., and Pattberg, P. (2019). The United Nations Framework Convention on Climate Change Secretariat as an orchestrator in global climate policymaking. *International Review of Administrative Sciences*, 0(0),1–18.

Hoffmann, M. J. (2011). *Climate Governance at the Crossroads: Experimenting with a Global Response After Kyoto*. New York: Oxford University Press.

Höhne, N. et al. (2017). The Paris Agreement: resolving the inconsistency between global goals and national contributions. *Climate Policy*, 17 (1),16–32.

Holden, E. (2019). Climate crisis will not be discussed at G7 next year, says Trump official. *The Guardian* [online]. 17 October 2019. www.theguardian.com/world/2019/oct/17/g7-summit-2020-trump-climate-crisis.

Ho-Lem, C., Zerriffi, H., and Kandlikar, M. (2011). Who participates in the Intergovernmental Panel on Climate Change and why: a quantitative assessment of the national representation of authors in the Intergovernmental Panel on Climate Change. *Global Environmental Change*, 21(4),1308–17.

Homer-Dixon, T. (2007). *The upside of down: catastrophe, creativity, and the renewal of civilization*. Toronto: Vintage Canada.

Hoppe, R., Wesselink, A., and Cairns, R. (2013). Lost in the problem: the role of boundary organisations in the governance of climate change. *WIREs Climate Change*, 4(4),283–300.

HSBC (2019). COP 25: Intransigence: renegotiating a 'pre-nup' after the wedding'. HSBC Global Research [online]. 16 December 2019. www.research.hsbc.com/C/1/1/339/S2Bzwn7.

Hsu, A., Moffat, A. S., Weinfurter, A. J., and Schwartz, J. D. (2015). Towards a new climate diplomacy. *Nature Climate Change*, 5, 501–3.

Hulme, M. (2009). *Why We Disagree About Climate Change. Understanding Controversy, Inaction and Opportunity*. Cambridge: Cambridge University Press.

Hunt, G. (Minister for the Environment) (2013). Streamlining government processes by dissolving the climate commission. Media release [online]. 19 September 2013. https://parlinfo.aph.gov.au/parlInfo/search/display/display.w3p;query=Id%3A%22media%2Fpressrel%2F2736602%22; src1=sm1.

IEA (2020). World energy balances: overview. Paris: International Energy Agency. www.iea.org/reports/world-energy-balances-overview.

IPCC (1990). *IPCC First Assessment Report. Policymaker Summary of Working Group I (Scientific Assessment of Climate Change)* [online]. Intergovernmental Panel on Climate Change (IPCC). www.ipcc.ch/site/ assets/uploads/2018/05/ipcc_90_92_assessments_far_wg_I_spm.pdf.

IPCC (2018a). Summary for policymakers. In V. Masson-Delmotte et al., eds., *Global warming of 1.5°C: An IPCC special report on the impacts of global warming of 1.5°C above pre-industrial levels and related global greenhouse gas emission pathways, in the context of strengthening the global response to the threat of climate change, sustainable development, and efforts to eradicate poverty.* Geneva: Intergovernmental Panel on Climate Change.

IPCC (2018b). *Summary for Policymakers of IPCC Special Report on Global Warming of 1.5°C approved by governments* [online]. 8 October 2018. Geneva: Intergovernmental Panel on Climate Change. www.ipcc.ch/2018/ 10/08/summary-for-policymakers-of-ipcc-special-report-on-global-warm ing-of-1-5 c-approved-by-governments/.

IPCC (n.d.). The Intergovernmental Panel on Climate Change – Homepage [online]. www.ipcc.ch/.

IPCC-TFI (n.d.). 2006 IPCC Guidelines for National Greenhouse Gas Inventories [online]. Intergovernmental Panel on Climate Change (IPCC) – Task Force on National Greenhouse Gas Inventories (TFI). www.ipcc-nggip .iges.or.jp/public/2006gl/index.html.

Isailovic, M., Widerberg, O., and Pattberg, P. (2013). Fragmentation of global environmental governance architectures: a literature review. IVM Institute for Environmental Studies, Report W-13/09 [online]. 1 July 2013. https:// research.vu.nl/ws/portalfiles/portal/804246/R13-09.pdf.

Ivanova, M. (2005). *Can the anchor hold? Rethinking the United Nations Environment Programme for the 21st Century.* Yale School of Forestry and Environmental Studies Publication Series, Report No. 7 [online]. September 2005. https://elischolar.library.yale.edu/fes-pubs/27/.

Ivanova, M. (2008). UNEP as anchor organization for the global environment. In F. Biermann, B. Siebenhüner and A. Schreyögg (eds.), *International Organizations in Global Environmental Governance.* Abington: Routledge, 151–73.

IVM (2015). *Non-state actors in a Paris Agreement: are cities and companies bridging the ambition gap?* [online]. Policy Brief. Amsterdam: Institute for Environmental Studies (IVM) and FORES. https://fores.se/wp-content/ uploads/2015/05/NSA_Policy_brief_Bonn2.pdf.

Jaeger, C. C., and Jaeger, J. (2011). Three views on two degrees. *Regional Environmental Change*, 11(1),15–26.

Jagers, S. C, . and Stripple, J. (2003). Climate governance beyond the state. *Global Governance*, 9(3),385–99.

James, R., Jones, R, . and Boyd, E. (2017). What is loss and damage from climate change? First academic study reveals different perspectives, challenging questions. *New Security Beat* [online]. 25 September 2017. www.news ecuritybeat.org/2017/09/loss-damage-climate-change-academic-study-reveals-perspectives-challenging-questions/.

Jamieson, D. (2014). *Reason in a Dark Time: Why the Struggle Against Climate Change Failed – and What It means for Our Future*. New York: Oxford University Press.

Johnson, D., and Levin, S. (2009). The tragedy of cognition: psychological biases and environmental inaction. *Current Science*, 97(11),1593–603.

Johnson, L., and Rampini, C. (2017). Are climate models global public goods? In D. Tyfield, R. Lave, S. Randalls and C. Thorpe, eds., *The Routledge Handbook of the Political Economy of Science*. London: Routledge, 263–74.

Johnson, P. M. (2001). Creating sustainable global governance. In J. J. Kirton, J. P. Daniels and A. Freytag, eds., *Guiding Global Order: G8 Governance in the Twenty-First Century*. Aldershot: Ashgate Publishing, 245–82.

Jordan, A. J., et al. (2015). Emergence of polycentric climate governance and its future prospects. *Nature Climate Change*, 5, 977–82.

Kapstein, E. B. (1999). Distributive justice as an international public good. a historical perspective. In I. Kaul, I. Grunberg and M. Stern, eds., *Global Public Goods: International Cooperation in the 21st Century*. Oxford: Oxford University Press, 88–115.

Karlsson-Vinkhuyzen, S., et al. (2017). Entry into force and then? The Paris agreement and state accountability. *Climate Policy*, 18(5),593–599.

Kaul, I. (2008). Providing (contested) global public goods. In V. Rittberger, M. Nettesheim and C. Huckel, eds., *Authority in the Global Political Economy*. Basingstoke and New York: Palgrave Macmillan, 89–115.

Kaul, I., and Blondin, D. (2016). Global oublic goods and the United Nations. In J. A. Ocampo, ed., *Global Governance and Development*. Oxford: Oxford University Press, 32–65.

Kaul, I., Conceição, P., Le Goulven, K., and Mendoza, R. U. (2003). Why do global public goods matter today? In I. Kaul, ed., *Providing Global Public Goods: Managing Globalization*. Oxford: Oxford University Press, 2–20.

Keck, M. E., and Sikkink. K. (1998). *Activists beyond Borders: Advocacy Networks in International Politics*. Ithaca, NY: Cornell University Press.

Keohane, R. O., and Victor, D. G. (2011). The regime complex for climate change. *Perspectives on Politics*, 9(1),7–23.

Keohane, R. O., and Victor, D. G. (2016). Cooperation and discord in global climate policy. *Nature Climate Change*, 6, 570–5.

Kirton, J. J., and Guebert, J. (2009). Climate change accountability: the G8's compliance record from 1975 to 2009. G8 Research Group [online]. 28 November 2009. www.g8.utoronto.ca/scholar/kirton-guebert-climate-091128.pdf.

Kirton, J. J., and Kikotsis, E. (2015). *The Global Governance of Climate Change: G7, G20, and UN Leadership*. Farnham: Ashgate.

Kokotsis, E. (2017). The Gx contribution to global climate governance. *StudiaDiplomatica*, 68(3),79–96.

Krasner, S. D. (1982). Structural causes and regime consequences: regimes as intervening variables. *International Organization*, 36(2),185–205

Kuo, L. (2020). China withheld data on coronavirus from WHO, recordings reveal. *The Guardian* [online]. 2 June 2020. www.theguardian.com/world/2020/jun/02/china-withheld-data-coronavirus-world-health-organization-recordings-reveal.

Kuramochi, T. et al. (2019). *Global climate action from cities, regions and businesses: Impact of individual actors and cooperative initiatives on global and national emissions* [online]. Second edition. NewClimate Institute, Data-Driven Lab, PBL, German Development Institute/Deutsches Institut für Entwicklungspolitik (DIE) and Blavatnik School of Government, University of Oxford. https://newclimate.org/wp-content/uploads/2019/09/Report-Global-Climate-Action-from-Cities-Regions-and-Businesses_2019.pdf.

Kuyper, J. W., Linnér, B.-O., and Schroeder, H. (2018). Non-state actors in hybrid global climate governance: justice, legitimacy, and effectiveness in a post-Paris era. *WIREs Climate Change*, 9(e497), 1–18.

Labatt, S., and White, R. R. (2007). *Carbon Finance: The Financial Implications of Climate Change*. Hoboken, NJ: John Wiley & Sons.

Larionova, M., and Kirton, J. J. (2015). *The G8-G20 relationship in global governance*. Farnham: Ashgate.

Lebada, A. M. (2019). UN Secretary-General presents 2020 Programme Budget, Reform Updates. *SDG Knowledge Hub* [online]. International Institute for Sustainable Development (IISD). 10 October 2019. https://sdg.iisd.org/news/un-secretary-general-presents-2020-programme-budget-reform-updates/.

Lebaron, G., and Lister, J. (2015). Benchmarking global supply chains: the power of the 'ethical audit' regime. *Review of International Studies*, 41 (5),905–24.

Lefeber, R., and Oberthür, S. (2012). Key features of the Kyoto Protocol's compliance system. In J. Brunnée, M. Doelle and L. Rajamani, eds., *Promoting Compliance in an Evolving Climate Regime*. Cambridge: Cambridge University Press, 77–101.

Lenton, T. M., et al. (2008). Tipping elements in the Earth's climate system. *PNAS*, 105(6),1786–93.

Lesnikowski, A., et al. (2017). What does the Paris Agreement mean for adaptation? *Climate Policy*, 17(7),825–31.

Levin, K., Cashore, B., Bernstein, S., and Auld, G. (2012). Overcoming the tragedy of super wicked problems. *Policy Sciences*, 45(2),123–52.

Lin, J. (2018). *Governing Climate Change: Global Cities and Transnational Lawmaking*. Cambridge: Cambridge University Press.

Livingstone, D. (2016). The G7 *climate mandate and tragedy of horizons*. Washington, DC: Carnegie Endowment for International Peace [online]. https://carnegieendowment.org/files/CP_263_Livingston_G7_Final.pdf/.

Magnan, A. K., and Ribera, T. (2016). Global adaptation after Paris. *Science*, 352(6291),1280–2.

Manguiat, M. S., and Raine, A. (2018). Strengthening national legal frameworks to implement the Paris Agreement. *Carbon & Climate Law Review*, 12 (1),15–22.

Marx, A., and Wouters, J. (2015). Competition and cooperation in the market of voluntary sustainability standards. In P. Delimatsis, ed., *The Law, Economics and Politics of International Standardisation*. Cambridge: Cambridge University Press, 215–41.

Mayrhofer, J. P., and Gupta, J. (2016). The science and politics of co-benefits in climate policy. *Environmental Science & Policy*, 57, 22–30.

McLeod, M. (2010). Private governance and climate change: institutional investors and emerging investor-driven governance mechanisms. *St Antony's International Review*, 5(2),46–65.

Mechler, R., et al. (2019). Science for loss and damage: findings and propositions. In R. Mechler et al., eds., *Loss and Damage from Climate Change: Concepts, Methods and Policy Options*. Cham: Springer, 3–37.

Merrill, L., and Funke, F. (2019). All change and no change: G20 commitment on fossil fuel subsidy reform, ten years on. SDG Knowledge Hub [online]. 3 October 2019. https://sdg.iisd.org/commentary/guest-articles/all-change-and-no-change-g20-commitment-on-fossil-fuel-subsidy-reform-ten-years-on/.

Mert, A. (2015). Public–private partnerships. In P. H. Pattberg and F. Zelli, eds., *Encyclopedia of Global Environmental Governance and Politics*. Cheltenham: Edward Elgar, 289–294.

Michaelowa, K., and Michaelowa, A. (2017). Transnational climate governance initiatives: designed for effective climate change mitigation? *International Interactions: Empirical and Theoretical Research in International Relations*, 43(1),129–55.

Minx, J. C., et al. (2017). Learning about climate change solutions in the IPCC and beyond. *Environmental Science & Policy*, 77, 252–9.

Najam, A., Papa, M., and Taiyab, N. (2006). *Global Environmental Governance: A Reform Agenda*. Winnipeg, Manitoba: International Institute for Sustainable Development [online]. www.iisd.org/pdf/2006/geg.pdf.

NAZCA (n.d.). Global Climate Action portal [online]. https://climateaction .unfccc.int/.

Norton, A. (2020). Coronavirus and climate change are two crises that need humanity to unite. *Climate Home News* [online]. 12 March 2020. www .climatechangenews.com/2020/03/12/coronavirus-climate-change-two-cri ses-need-humanity-unite/.

Nyman, J., and Stainforth, T. (2018). Talanoa Dialogue: a new approach to global decision making or a rebranding of business as usual? [online]. Institute for European Environmental Policy. 4 July 2018. https://ieep.eu/ news/talanoa-dialogue-a-new-approach-to-global-decision-making-or- a-rebranding-of-business-as-usual.

Obergassel, W. et al., (2019). *Paris Agreement: Ship Moves out of the Drydock. An Assessment of COP-24 in Katowice*. Wuppertal: Wuppertal Institute [online]. wupperinst.org/fa/redaktion/downloads/publications/COP-24- Report.pdf.

Oberthür, S. (2011). The European Union's performance in the international climate change regime. *Journal of European Integration*, 33(6),667–82.

Odionu, G. (2019). *Striking the right balance: climate finance for developing countries*. Oxford Business Law Blog [online]. Oxford: University of Oxford, Faculty of Law. 27 March 2019. www.law.ox.ac.uk/business-law- blog/blog/2019/03/striking-right-balance-climate-finance-developing- countries.

OECD (2019). *Climate finance for developing countries reached USD 71 billion in 2017. 13 September 2019*. Paris: Organisation for Economic Co-operation and Development (OECD) [online]. www.oecd.org/environment/climate- finance-for-developing-countries-reached-usd-71-billion-in-2017.htm.

Orr, S. K. (2016). Institutional control and climate change activism at COP 21 in Paris. *Global Environmental Politics*, 16(3),23–30.

Ostrom, E., Burger, J., Field, C. B., Norgaard, R. B., and Policansky, D. (1999). Revisiting the commons: local lessons, global challenges. *Science*, 284 (5412), 278–82.

Paavola, J. (2012). Climate change: the ultimate tragedy of the Commons? In D. H. Cole and E. Ostrom, eds., *Property in Land and Other Resources.* Cambridge, MA: Lincoln Institute of Land Policy, 417–33.

Paavola, J. (2019). Climate as a commons. In B. Hudson, J. Rosenbloom and D. Cole, eds., *Routledge Handbook of the Study of the Commons.* London: Routledge, 188–97.

Pattberg, P. (2010). Public–private partnerships in global climate governance. *Wiley Interdisciplinary Reviews: Climate Change,* 1(2),279–87.

Pattberg, P. (2017). The emergence of carbon disclosure: exploring the role of governance entrepreneurs. *Environment and Planning C: Politics and Space,* 35(8),1437–55.

Pattberg, P., and Stripple, J. (2008). Beyond the public and private divide: remapping transnational climate governance in the 21st century. *International Environmental Agreements: Politics, Law and Economics,* 8(4),367–88.

Pattberg, P., and Widerberg, O. (2016). Transnational multistakeholder partnerships for sustainable development: Conditions for success. *Ambio,* 45 (1),42–51.

Pattberg, P., and Widerberg, O. (2017). The climate change regime. In *Oxford Research Encyclopedia: Climate Science.* Oxford: Oxford University Press.

Pegram, T. (2020). Coronavirus is a failure of global governance – now the world needs a radical transformation. *The Conversation* [online]. 5 May 2020. https://theconversation.com/coronavirus-is-a-failure-of-glo bal-governance-now-the-world-needs-a-radical-transformation-136535.

Persson, Å. (2019). Global adaptation governance: an emerging but contested domain. *WIREs Climate Change,* 10(4),1–18.

Persson, Å. , and Dzebo, A. (2019). Special issue: exploring global and transnational governance of climate change adaptation. *International Environmental Agreements: Politics, Law and Economics,* 19, 357–67.

Peters, G. B. (2005). The problem of policy problems. *Journal of Comparative Policy Analysis: Research and Practice,* 7(4),349–70.

Pickering, J., and Rübbelke, D. (2014). International cooperation on adaptation to climate change. In A. Markandya, I. Galarraga and E. Sainz de Murieta, eds., *Routledge Handbook of the Economics of Climate Change Adaptation.* London: Routledge, 56–75

Pielke, R. Jr., Prins, G., Rayner, S., and Sarewitz, D. (2007). Lifting the taboo on adaptation. *Nature,* 445, 597–98.

Rademaekers, K., et al. (2019). *Study on Energy Prices, Costs and Subsidies and their Impact on Industry and Households.* Trinomics/European Union.

Rajamani, L. (2016a). The 2015 Paris Agreement: interplay between hard, soft and non-obligations. *Journal of Environmental Law*, 28(2),337–58.

Rajamani, L. (2016b). Ambition and differentiation in the 2015 Paris Agreement: interpretative possibilities and underlying politics. *International & Comparative Law Quarterly*, 65(2),493–514.

Rajamani, L., and Werksman, J. (2018). The legal character and operational relevance of the Paris Agreement's temperature goal. *Philosophical Transactions of the Royal Society*, A 376: 20160458.

Rajamani. L., and Brunnée, J. (2017). The legality of downgrading nationally determined contributions under the Paris Agreement: lessons from the US disengagement. *Journal of Environmental Law*, 29(3),537–51.

Raustiala, K., and Victor, D. G. (2004). The regime complex for plant genetic resources. *International Organization*, 58(2),277–309.

Rayner, T., and Jordan, A. (2016). Climate change policy in the European Union. In T. Rayner and A. Jordan (eds.), *Oxford Research Encyclopedia of Climate Science*. Oxford: Oxford University Press, 1–31.

Reynolds, J., and Wagner, G. (2018). *Governance of highly decentralized non-state actors: the case of solar geoengineering*. Discussion Paper, Harvard Kennedy School Belfer Center [online]. www.belfercenter.org/publication/gov ernance-highly-decentralized-nonstate-actors-case-solar-geoengineering.

Roberts, J. T., Natson, S., Hoffmeister, V., et al. (2017). How will we pay for loss and damage? *Ethics, Policy, and Environment*, 20(2),208–26.

Roger, C. B. (2020). *The Origins of Informality: Why the Legal Foundations of Global Governance are Shifting, and Why It Matters*. Oxford: Oxford University Press.

Savage, K., and Hope, M. (2019). Global climate coalition: documents show how a fossil fuel lobby group manipulated UN climate negotiations. *Climate Liability News* [online]. 25 April 2019. www.climateliabilitynews.org/2019/ 04/25/global-climate-coalition-gcc-un-climate-change-ipcc/.

Schinko, T., Mechler, R.ç and Hochrainer-Stigler, S. (2019). The risk and policy space for loss and damage: integrating notions of distributive and compensa-tory justice with comprehensive climate risk management. In R. Mechler et al., eds., *Loss and Damage from Climate Change: Concepts, Methods and Policy Options*. Cham: Springer, 83–110.

Schipper, E. L. F. (2006). Conceptual history of adaptation in the UNFCCC process. *RECIEL*, 15(1),82–92.

SDG Knowledge Platform (n.d.). Sustainable development Goal 17. Division for Sustainable Development Goals (DSDG) in the United Nations Department of Economic and Social Affairs (UNDESA) [online]. https:// sustainabledevelopment.un.org/sdg17.

Setzer, J.ç and Byrnes, R. (2019). *Global trends in climate change litigation: 2019 snapshot*. London: Grantham Research Institute on Climate Change and the Environment and the Centre for Climate Change Economics and Policy [online]. July 2019. www.lse.ac.uk/GranthamInstitute/wp-content/uploads/2019/07/ GRI_Global-trends-in-climate-change-litigation-2019-snapshot-2.pdf.

Sharma, A. (2017). Precaution and post-caution in the Paris Agreement: adaptation, loss and damage and finance. *Climate Policy*, 17(1),33–47.

Shaw, C. (2017). The two degrees celsius limit. In *Oxford Research Encyclopedia of Climate. Science*. Oxford: Oxford University Press.

Shell (n.d.). Our response to climate change [online]. www.shell.co.uk/ a-cleaner-energy-future/our-response-to-climate-change.html.

Singh, N., Finnegan, J., and Levin, K. (2016). MRV 101: *Understanding measurement, reporting, and verification of climate change mitigation*. WRI Working Paper. Washington DC: World Resources Institute [online]. wriorg.s3.amazonaws.com/s3fs-public/MRV_101_0.pdf.

Skjærseth, J. B. (2017). The Commission's shifting climate leadership: from emissions trading to energy union. In R. K. W. Wurzel, J. Connelly and D. Liefferink, eds., *The European Union in International Climate Politics: Still Taking a Lead?* Abingdon and New York: Routledge, 37–51.

Skovgaard, J. (2014). EU climate policy after the crisis. *Environmental Politics*, 23(1),1–17.

Slaughter, A.-M. (2015). The Paris Approach to global governance. *Project Syndicate*. [online]. 28 December 2015. www.project-syndicate.org/commen tary/paris-agreement-model-for-global-governance-by-anne-marie-slaughter-2015–12.

Smeds, E., and Acuto, M. (2018). Networking cities after Paris: weighing the ambition of urban climate change experimentation. *Global Policy*, 9(4),549–59.

Smith, J. J., and Tanveer, A. M. (2018). Globalization's vehicle: the evolution and future of emission regulation in the ICAO and IMO in comparative assessment. *Climate Law*, 8(1–2),70–103.

Snowden, D. J., and Boone, M. E. (2007). A leader's framework for decision making. *Harvard Business Review*, 1–9.

Sørensen, E., and Torfing, J. (2009). Managing governance networks effective and democratic through metagovernance. *Public Administration*, 87 (2),234–58.

SRU (n.d.). Mission. German Advisory Council on the Environment (SRU). Online: www.umweltrat.de/EN/council/council_node.html.

Stern, N. (2007). *The Economics of Climate Change: The Stern Review*. Cambridge: Cambridge University Press.

Streck, C., von Unger, M., and Krämer, N. (2019). From Paris to Katowice: COP-24 tackles the Paris Rulebook. *Journal for European Environmental Planning Law*, 16, 165–190.

Tamma, P., Schaart, E., and Gurzu, A. (2019). Europe's Green Deal plan unveiled. *Politico* [online]. 12 December 2019. www.politico.eu/article/the-commissions-green-deal-plan-unveiled/.

Taylor, M., and Watts, J. (2019). Revealed: the 20 firms behind a third of all carbon emissions. *The Guardian* [online]. 9 October 2019. www.theguardian.com/environment/2019/oct/09/revealed-20-firms-third-carbon-emissions.

Terman, R., and Voeten, E. (2018). The relational politics of shame: evidence from the universal periodic review. *Review of International Organizations*, 13 (1),1–23.

Thatcher, M., and Coen, D. (2008). Reshaping European regulatory space: an evolutionary analysis. *West European Politics*, 31(4),806–36.

The Climate Group (2018). Leading states and regions decarbonizing at double the rate of G20 governments [online]. www.theclimategroup.org/news/leading-states-and-regions-decarbonizing-double-rate-g20-governments.

The Economist (2015). *The Cost of Inaction: Recognising the Value at Risk from Climate Change*. London: The Economist Intelligence Unit [online]. https://eiuperspectives.economist.com/sites/default/files/The%20cost%20of%20inaction_0.pdf.

The White House (2014). U.S.–China Joint Announcement on Climate Change [online]. 11 November 2014. https://obamawhitehouse.archives.gov/the-press-office/2014/11/11/us-china-joint-announcement-climate-change.

Thornton, T. F., and Comberti, C. (2017). Synergies and trade-offs between adaptation, mitigation and development. *Climatic Change*, 140(1),5–18.

Timmons, R. J. (2011). Multipolarity and the new world (dis)order: US hegemonic decline and the fragmentation of the global climate regime. *Global Environmental Change*, 21(3),776–84.

Timperley, J. (2019). COP-25: What was achieved and where to next? *Climate Home News* [online]. 16 December 2019. www.climatechangenews.com/2019/12/16/cop25-achieved-next/.

Torny, D. (2017). If at first you don't succeed: the development of climate change legislation in Ireland. *Irish Political Studies*, 32(2),247–67.

UK Government (2008). Climate Change Act 2008 [online]. www.legislation.gov.uk/ukpga/2008/27/contents.

Umbers, L. M., and Moss, J. (2019). The climate duties of sub-national political communities. *Political Studies*, 1–17.

United Nations (1992). *United Nations Framework Convention on Climate Change*. FCCC/INFORMAL/84 [online]. https://unfccc.int/resource/docs/convkp/conveng.pdf.

United Nations (2012). The future we want. Outcome document of the United Nations conference on sustainable development. Rio de Janeiro, Brazil, 20–22 June 2012 [online]. https://sustainabledevelopment.un.org/content/documents/733FutureWeWant.pdf.

United Nations (2015). COP21: UN chief hails new climate change agreement as 'monumental triumph'. UN News [online]. 12 December 2015. https://news.un.org/en/story/2015/12/517982-cop21-un-chief-hails-new-climate-change-agreement-monumental-triumph.

United Nations (2020). UN tackles 'infodemic' of misinformation and cybercrime in COVID-19 crisis. United Nations Department of Global Communications [online]. 31 March 2020. www.un.org/en/un-coronavirus-communications-team/un-tackling-%E2%80%98infodemic%E2%80%99-misinformation-and-cybercrime-covid-19.

UN DESA (2019). World Urbanization Prospects: The 2018 Revision (ST/ESA/SER.A/420). New York: United Nations Department of Economic and Social Affairs, Population Division [online]. https://population.un.org/wup/Publications/Files/WUP2018-Report.pdf.

UN News (2014). Climate Summit: 'All hands on deck' declares Ban, calling for leadership, concrete action [online]. 23 September 2014. https://news.un.org/en/story/2014/09/478172-climate-summit-all-hands-deck-declares-ban-calling-leadership-concrete-action.

UNEP (2012). United Nations Environment Programme upgraded to universal membership following Rio+20 Summit. Press Release. Nairobi: United Nations Environment Programme [online]. 21 December 2012. www.unenvironment.org/news-and-stories/press-release/united-nations-environment-programme-upgraded-universal-membership.

UNEP (2018). Emissions Gap Report 2018. Nairobi: United Nations Environment Programme [online]. wedocs.unep.org/bitstream/handle/20.500.11822/27114/AGR_2018.pdf/.

UNFCCC (1998). *Kyoto Protocol to the United Nations Framework Convention on Climate Change*. United Nations Framework Convention on Climate Change [online]. https://unfccc.int/sites/default/files/kpeng.pdf.

UNFCCC (2008). Report of the Conference of the Parties on its thirteenth session, held in Bali from 3 to 15 December 2007. Addendum. FCCC/CP/2007/6/Add.1. United Nations Framework Convention on Climate Change [online]. https://unfccc.int/resource/docs/2007/cop13/eng/06a01.pdf.

UNFCCC (2015). *The Paris Agreement.* United Nations Framework Convention on Climate Change [online]. https://unfccc.int/sites/default/files/english_paris_agreement.pdf.

UNFCCC (2016). Decision 1/CP.21. Adoption of the Paris Agreement. FCCC/CP/2015/10/Add. 29 January 2016. United Nations Framework Convention on Climate Change [online]. https://unfccc.int/resource/docs/2015/cop21/eng/10a01.pdf#page=2.

UNFCCC (2018). Talanoa Call for Action. United Nations Framework Convention on Climate Change [online]. https://unfccc.int/sites/default/files/resource/Talanoa%20Call%20for%20Action.pdf.

UNFCCC (2019a). Statement by the UN Secretary-General António Guterres on the outcome of COP25 [online]. 15 December 2019. https://unfccc.int/news/statement-by-the-un-secretary-general-antonio-guterres-on-the-outcome-of-cop25.

UNFCCC (2019b). Fact Sheet. The UNFCCC Programme Budget 2020–21. United Nations Climate Change Secretariat. https://unfccc.int/sites/default/files/resource/Budget-2020–2021-fact-sheet.pdf.

UNFCCC (2019c). Report of the Conference of the Parties serving as the meeting of the Parties to the Paris Agreement on the third part of its first session, held in Katowice from 2 to 15 December 2018. 19 March 2019. FCCC/PA/CMA/2018/3/Add.2. United Nations Framework Convention on Climate Change [online]. https://unfccc.int/sites/default/files/resource/cma2018_3_add2_new_advance.pdf#page=18.

UNFCCC (2020). Open Letter by the Executive Secretary on COVID-19. United Nations Climate Change [online]. 23 April 2020. https://unfccc.int/news/open-letter-by-the-executive-secretary-on-covid-19.

UNFCCC (n.d.a). Regional Centres and Networks. United Nations Framework Convention on Climate Change [online]. https://unfccc.int/process-and-meetings/bodies/constituted-bodies/adaptation-committee-ac/areas-of-work/regional-centres-and-networks#eq-5.

UNFCCC (n.d.b).What is transparency and reporting? United Nations Framework Convention on Climate Change [online]. https://unfccc.int/process-and-meetings/transparency-and-reporting/the-big-picture/what-is-transparency-and-reporting.

UNFCCC (n.d.c). Marrakech Partnership for Global Climate Action. United Nations Framework Convention on Climate Change [online]. https://unfccc.int/climate-action/marrakech-partnership-for-global-climate-action.

UNFCCC (n.d.d). Marrakech Partnership at COP-23. United Nations Framework Convention on Climate Change [online]. https://unfccc.int/climate-action/marrakech-partnership/events/marrakech-partnership-at-cop23.

UNFCCC Clearinghouse (n.d.). Fiji Clearing House for Risk Transfer. Homepage. United Nations Framework Convention on Climate Change [online]. http://unfccc-clearinghouse.org/.

UNGA (1988). Resolution 43/53: Protection of global climate for present and future generations of mankind. A/RES/43/53, 6 December 1988. United Nations General Assembly [online]. www.un.org/documents/ga/res/43/a43r053.htm.

UN Secretary General (2020). Secretary-General's Nelson Mandela lecture: 'tackling the inequality pandemic: a new social contract for a new Era' [as delivered]. 18 July 2020 [online]. www.un.org/sg/en/content/sg/statement/2020–07-18/secretary-generals-nelson-mandela-lecture-%E2%80%9Ctackling-the-inequality-pandemic-new-social-contract-for-new-era%E2%80%9D-delivered.

US Department of State (2019). On the U.S. withdrawal from the Paris Agreement. Michael R. Pompeo, Secretary of State. 4 November 2019 [online]. www.state.gov/on-the-u-s-withdrawal-from-the-paris-agreement/.

Vabulas, F. (2019). The importance of informal intergovernmental organizations: a typology of transnational administration without independent secretariats. In D. Stone and K. Moloney, eds., *The Oxford Handbook of Global Policy and Transnational Administration.* Oxford: Oxford University Press, 401–18.

Vabulas, F., and Snidal, D. (2013). Organization without delegation: informal intergovernmental organizations (IIGOs) and the spectrum of intergovernmental arrangements. *The Review of International Organizations,* 8(2),193–220.

Van Asselt, H. (2007). Dealing with the Fragmentation of Global Climate Governance. Legal and Political Approaches in Interplay Management Management. *Global Governance Working Paper,* No. 30, May 2007. The Global Governance Project [online]. www.peacepalacelibrary.nl/ebooks/files/C08-0093-Asselt-Dealing.pdf.

Van Asselt, H. (2011). Legal and political approaches in interplay management: dealing with the fragmentation of global climate governance. In S. Oberthür and O. S. Stokke, eds., *Managing Institutional Complexity: Regime Interplay and Global Environmental Change.* Cambridge, MA and London: MIT Press, 59–86.

Van Asselt, H. (2014). *Alongside the UNFCCC: Complementary Venues for Climate Action.* Center for Climate and Energy Solutions (C2ES) [online]. www.c2es.org/site/assets/uploads/2014/05/alongside-unfccc-complementary-venues-climate-action.pdf.

Van der Heijden, J., Patterson, J., Juhola, S., and Wolfram, M. (2018). Special section: advancing the role of cities in climate governance – promise, limits, politics. *Journal of Environmental Planning and Management*, 62 (3),365–73.

Van der Lugt, C., and Dingwerth, K. (2015). Governing where focality is low: UNEP and the Principles for Responsible Investment. In K. Abbott, P. Genschel, D. Snidal and B. Zangl, eds., *International Organizations as Orchestrators*. Cambridge: Cambridge University Press, 237–61.

Vandenbergh, M. P., and Gilligan, J. M. (2017). *Beyond Politics: The Private Governance Response to Climate Change.* Cambridge: Cambridge University Press.

Vanhala, L., and Hestbaek, C. (2016). Framing climate change loss and damage in UNFCCC negotiations. *Global Environmental Politics*, 16(4),111–29.

Van Schaik, L., and Schunz, S. (2012). Explaining EU activism and impact in global climate politics: is the union a norm- or interest-driven actor? *Journal of Common Market Studies*, 50(1),169–86.

Verkuijl, C., and van Asselt, H. (2019). Paris rules? *Environmental Policy and Law*, 49(1),11–19.

Victor, D. (2009). Plan B for Copenhagen. *Nature*, 461(7262),342–4.

Victor, D. G., Geels, F. W., and Sharpe, S. (2019). Accelerating the low carbon transition: The case for stronger, more targeted and coordinated international action. Brookings [online]. www.energy-transitions.org/sites/default/files/ Accelerating-The-Transitions_Report.pdf.

Vidal, J. (2010). Copenhagen climate failure blamed on 'Danish text'. *The Guardian* [online]. 31 May 2010. www.theguardian.com/environment/ 2010/may/31/climate-change-copenhagen-danish-text.

Vogler, J. (2018). Energy, climate change, and global governance: the 2015 Paris Agreement in perspective. In D. J. Davidson and M. Gross, eds., *Oxford Handbook of Energy and Society*. Oxford: Oxford University Press.

Voigt, C., and Ferreira, F. (2016). Differentiation in the Paris Agreement. *Climate Law*, 6(1–2),58–74.

Von Bassewitz, N. (2013). International climate change policy: where do we Stand? In O. C. Ruppel, C. Roschmann and K. Ruppel-Schlichting, eds., *Climate Change: International Law and Global Governance: Volume II: Policy, Diplomacy and Governance in a Changing Environment*. Baden-Baden: Nomos Verlagsgesellschaft mbH, 101–70.

Voosen, P. (2009). Creative accounting will help E.U. meet Kyoto targets. *New York Times* [online]. 13 November 2009. https://archive.nytimes .com/www.nytimes.com/gwire/2009/11/13/13greenwire-creative-account ing-will-help-eu-meet-kyoto-cl-27564.html?pagewanted=all.

Waldman, S. (2019). Climate preparation report released by panel previously disbanded by Trump. *Climate Wire* [online]. 4 April 2019. www.scientifica

merican.com/article/climate-preparation-report-released-by-panel-previ ously-disbanded-by-trump/.

Watts, J., and Doherty, B. (2018). US and Russia ally with Saudi Arabia to water down climate pledge. *The Guardian* [online]. 9 December 2018. www.the guardian.com/environment/2018/dec/09/us-russia-ally-saudi-arabia-water- down-climate-pledges-un.

Watts, J. (2019). US and Saudi Arabia blocking regulation of geoengineering, sources say. *The Guardian* [online]. 18 March 2019. www.theguardian.com/ environment/2019/mar/18/us-and-saudi-arabia-blocking-regulation-of-geo engineering-sources-say.

Weart, S. R. (2008). *The Discovery of Global Warming*. Revised and Expanded Edition. Cambridge, MA: Harvard University Press.

Weaver, S., Lötjönen, S., and Ollikainen, M. (2019). *Overview of National Climate Change Advisory Councils*. The Finnish Climate Change Panel, Report 3/2019 [online]. www.ilmastopaneeli.fi/wp-content/uploads/2019/ 05/Overview-of-national-CCCs.pdf.

Wei, D. (2016). Linking non-state action with the U.N. Framework Convention on Climate Change. Arlington, VA: Center for Climate and Energy Solutions (C2ES) [online]. www.c2es.org/site/assets/uploads/2016/10/linking-non state-action-unfccc.pdf.

Widerberg, O. (2016). Mapping institutional complexity in the Anthropocene: a network approach. In P. Pattberg and F. Zelli, eds., *Environmental Politics and Governance in the Anthropocene: Institutions and Legitimacy in a Complex World*. London, UK: Routledge, 81–102.

Widerberg, O. E., Pattberg, P. H., and Kristensen, K. E. G. (2016). *Mapping the Institutional Architecture of Global Climate Change Governance V.2*. Institute for Environmental Studies/IVM.

Willsher, K., Borger, J., and Holmes, O. (2020). US accused of 'modern piracy' after diversion of masks meant for Europe. *The Guardian* [online]. 4 April 2020. www.theguardian.com/world/2020/apr/03/mask-wars-corona virus-outbidding-demand.

Wirth, D. A. (2015). The Eenvironment. In J. Cogan, I. Hurd and I. Johnstone, eds., *Oxford Handbook of International Organizations*. Oxford: Oxford University Press, 425–46.

Wurzel, R. K. W., Liefferink, D., and Di Lullo, M. (2019). The European Council, the Council and the Member States: changing environmental leadership dynamics in the European Union. *Environmental Politics*, 28(2),248–270.

Yamin, F., and Depledge, J. (2004). *The International Climate Change Regime: A Guide to Rules, Institutions and Procedures*. Cambridge: Cambridge University Press.

Yeo, S. (2013). Australia Climate Commission starts fightback against Abbott cuts. *Climate Home News* [online]. 24 September 2013. www.climatechange news.com/2013/09/24/climate-commission-fights-back-as-abbotts-onslaught-gets-underway/.

Young, O. R. (2008). The architecture of global environmental governance: bringing science to bear on policy. *Global Environmental Politics*, 8(1),14–32.

Zhang, Y.-X., Chao, Q.-C., Zheng, Q.-H., and Huang, L. (2017). The withdrawal of the U.S. from the Paris Agreement and its impact on global climate change governance. *Advances in Climate Change Research*, 8(4),213–19.

Zito, A. R., Burns, C., and Lenschow, A. (2019). Is the trajectory of European Union environmental policy less certain? *Environmental Politics*, 28 (2),187–207.

Acknowledgements

The analysis presented here has greatly benefited from comments and suggestions by colleagues involved in the GLOBE project and we would like to especially thank: Charlie Roger, Adam Holesch, Jacint Jordana, David Levi-Faur, Axel Marx, Angel Saz-Carranza, Marie Vandendriessche, Jan Wouters and Michael Zürn. Special thanks also go to Kristin Higgins for her invaluable research assistance. Finally, the Element was completed during the extraordinary COVID-19 lockdown across London and the UK and we would like to dedicate this Element to all of our parents and close family who we Skyped and phoned during this difficult time. Specifically, David wishes to thank his wonderful wife Natasha for being so supportive and two beautiful girls, Alexandria and Florence, who are a wonderful reason to take a break from writing. Tom thanks his partner Sora for her serenity and humor during these strange times, and Julia thanks Herbert, Angela, Christina and Alex who provided encouragement and support via Skype and in person.

Funding Information

This Element was supported by the GLOBE project (Global Governance and the European Union: Future Trends and Scenarios), funded by the European Commission's Horizon 2020 program. GLOBE addresses the issues defined as strategic priorities in the 2016 EU Global Strategy – trade, development, security and climate change – as well as migration and global finance, in order to identify the major roadblocks to effective and coherent global governance by multiple stakeholders in a multipolar world. This Element also benefited from the support of the Global Governance Institute (GGI) at University College London, a university-wide initiative, promoting cross-disciplinary research and informed public debate on possible solutions to global societal challenges.

Cambridge Elements ≡

Public and Nonprofit Administration

Andrew Whitford
University of Georgia
Andrew Whitford is Alexander M. Crenshaw Professor of Public Policy in the School of Public and International Affairs at the University of Georgia. His research centers on strategy and innovation in public policy and organization studies.

Robert Christensen
Brigham Young University
Robert Christensen is professor and George Romney Research Fellow in the Marriott School at Brigham Young University. His research focuses on prosocial and antisocial behaviors and attitudes in public and nonprofit organizations.

About the Series
The foundation of this series are cutting-edge contributions on emerging topics and definitive reviews of keystone topics in public and nonprofit administration, especially those that lack longer treatment in textbook or other formats. Among keystone topics of interest for scholars and practitioners of public and nonprofit administration, it covers public management, public budgeting and finance, nonprofit studies, and the interstitial space between the public and nonprofit sectors, along with theoretical and methodological contributions, including quantitative, qualitative and mixed-methods pieces.

The Public Management Research Association
The Public Management Research Association improves public governance by advancing research on public organizations, strengthening links among interdisciplinary scholars, and furthering professional and academic opportunities in public management.

Cambridge Elements ⹀

Public and Nonprofit Administration

Printed in the United States
By Bookmasters